A Safe Landing Place for Kamikaze Kids

Growing up has always been a high-risk activity. But the self-destructive behavior of contemporary teens threatens to place America's most valuable resource on the list of endangered species.

And teenagers are getting a lot of unneeded help from the other side of 30. Adults have booby trapped the teen years with all kinds of pitfalls: drugs, booze, AIDS, a poisoned atmosphere, stray bullets, AWOL parents. No wonder so many of you act like there's no tomorrow!

If you're singing those *"Nothing-To-Live-For Teenage Blues,"* open this book and start taking charge of your future. The time for feeling hopeless and helpless is past.

Readers' Reviews

Can a book intended for teenage eyes survive the praise of parents, much less teachers and probation officers? You decide...

Thanks from teens

"It's so simple, even older people would get a lot out of it." Ann, 18, Jacksonville, Florida

"It's the best book I ever read in my entire life (all 16 years of it)." Miriam, Atlantic Beach, New York

"...it's helped me understand myself and my friends better." Sue, 15, Glendale, California

"I used it for a book report and got my first A+." Scott, Calistoga, California

"The waters are still rough, but now I've learned to sail with the current without worrying about every wave." Keisita, 18, Kjaerarsvej, Denmark

"For the first time I understand my parents." Freida, 15, Sedona, Arizona

"Guess what – I got kicked out of Algebra for reading your book!" Thad, 17, Farmington, New Mexico

Praise from parents

"The manual did what two college degrees, 15 years of professional experience, a couple of marriages and 38 years of living failed to accomplish." Mrs SW, San Antonio, Texas

"I wish to heaven I had something like this 40 years ago." Mr GJ, San Francisco, California

"There's so much love in this house since we read the book." Mrs SC, Jr, Memphis, Tennessee

"After our 16-year-old left home, she got a copy of the Teenage Survival Manual and now she's back. It's a whole new beginning. Thank you, thank you, thank you." Mrs GW, Nevada City, California

"I woke up and found my husband finishing your manual, at 3:00 A.M. He wants to order 12 copies..." EH, Key West, Florida

"I had forgotten how it was to be 16 when nobody trusts you. [The book] really helped me be with my kids." Mrs SS, Monterey, California

"You don't treat teenagers like a disease only time will cure." Mrs SWC, Sacramento, California

"It helped us cope with several crises." Mr and Mrs EL, Ann Arbor, Michigan

"Please send 6 copies – we want to share the book with other families." HL, MD, Denver, Colorado

"I walked into my daughter's room late last night thinking she was sneaking tube time, and found her locked into your book. That's never happened before." BP, Palo Alto, California

Testimonials from teachers

"By far the best book written for teenagers…" Mrs LR, San Marcos, California

"This book should be part of every high school curriculum in the US." Ms LAM, Yonkers, New York

"I want to purchase a copy for every student in my Alternate program." HH, Palos Verdes, California

"After considerable agonizing with our principal and PTA, I received permission to use the manual in my Senior Problems classes. The kids are wild about it." Ms PP, St Louis, Missouri

"Why don't you get our school district to put this book in the libraries?" Mr JL, Chicago, Illinois

"…with only 6 copies to go around, the students actually fight over who gets to take one home." Mrs KH, West Los Angeles, California

Plaudits from professionals

"We've been using the manual with great success for rap sessions with counselors, mental health workers, teachers and teens." JLR, MSW (A Southwest Counseling Service)

"This looks to be a special book that would help me 'see' what some of my kids are going through." KJH, Juvenile Division, Ninth Judicial District Court, Douglas Co., Nevada

"Many teachers, church groups, parent counseling classes in the lodge find this book answers their needs so well." VP, Workshop Director, Anaheim, California

"Your book is required reading before granting probation." DTB, MSW, Delaware County Juvenile Detention Center, Pennsylvania

"For several years now, our chapters have used your book to nurture young people's spiritual education, leadership skills and a sense of who and what they are..." TP, Coordinator, International Youth of Unity (YOU), Missouri

"Keep writing. You have your pulse on the teenage phenomenon." LF, United Methodist Church, Washington

"...it helps the kids survive Alaska's long winters." LH, Norton Sound Health Corp.

Raves from reviewers

"I was skeptical...thought it would be loose and compromising but was pleasantly, gratefully surprised. It's an important book – clear, passionate."—Guru RKK, Sikh Youth Federation of Canada, Editor, *New Directions*.

"I can't tell you how impressed I am with your approach. I'll crib big chunks for my show." PH, Talkshow Host, California

TEENAGE
SURVIVAL
MANUAL

How to Reach 20 in One Piece
(And Enjoy Every Step of the Journey)

A New Edition
by H Samm Coombs

A Discovery Book

Library of Congress Cataloging-in-Publication Data
Coombs, H. Samm. 1928-
Teenage survival manual : how to reach "20" in
one piece (and enjoy every step of the journey) /
by H. Samm Coombs. --A new ed.
    240 p.   21.5 cm.
    Includes index.
    ISBN 0-925258-08-3 : $9.95
    1. Teenagers--Conduct of life. 2. Self-reali-
zation--Juvenile literature. 3. New Age movement-
-Juvenile literature.
I. Title.
BJ1661.C64   1989   248.8'3--dc20   89-7851   CIP

TEENAGE SURVIVAL MANUAL

Published by: Discovery Books, Inc.,
7282 Sir Francis Drake Blvd P.O. Box 410, Lagunitas, CA 94938

Printed in the United States of America

First edition published 1977
Second edition published 1978,
    Reprinted 1979
Third edition published 1981,
    Reprinted 1983, 1985, 1988;
Fourth edition published 1989.

Current edition's most recent printing is indicated by the first digit below:
2 3 4 5 6 7 8

Dedication

To my helpmate, Shirley Coombs,
and Tom Perine, Tom James,
Jerry Fogelson, Mrs Elvidge,
Hedda Lark, Mr Littlejohn,
sages past and present,
and that singular person who is my mother.

Acknowledgements

Thank you
Dick Moore and Stephanie Lipney for your illustrations,
Dan Van Zyle for your cover design,
Scott Coombs for your proof-reading
and editorial assistance,
Desktop Publishing, Inc. for your professional assistance,
Jefferson Coombs for your 'street smarts'
and Devil's Advocacy,
and librarians and booksellers for the spaces in your places.

One ship drives east
and another drives west
With the selfsame
winds that blow.
'Tis the set of the sails
and not the gales
Which tells us the way to go.

Winds of Fate

Ella Wheeler Wilcox

Table of Contents

Contents

Contents

Author's Preface

The reader might well ask the author, "What motivates a grown-up to write a book about growing up?"

No voice in the night commanded me. I have no guru to placate, no church to fill or cult to cultivate. But I do have a son who is approaching his teens as this is being written. Like most fathers, I feel called on to raise a torch to help him steer clear of the pitfalls I have met along life's path.

Also involved is the conviction that human history might stop repeating itself if just one generation were to grow up conscious of what makes man super. Once aware of this power, the acts and armor inherited from the past can be shed, without feeling threatened.

I do not mean to suggest this book will usher in the Aquarian Age. But it's a step in the right direction, aimed as it is at the people who will crew Spaceship Earth through the next century. A teenager is a lot closer to making his/her life work than are most adults; closer by virtue of not having had time to go far wrong. The beginning is a very good place to get started – on the right foot.

H Samm Coombs
Lagunitas, California

Firstword

Congratulations.

By opening this book you've shut a lot of mouths that have been telling the world it's impossible to communicate with teenagers unless the message is carried on prime time TV or buried in the lyric of a Top 40 tune.

Of course, opening a book is not finishing it. But, "a journey of a thousand miles begins with the first step," which you have just taken! Now may we suggest a way to get through the upcoming pages. There's no rush – this isn't some kind of assignment. Place your 'manual' next to your bed and chew on a chapter before ZZZzzzing. Ideas are more digestible when you're horizontal. And the alpha waves your brain generates on the threshold of sleep have a way of making invisible things like ideas meaningful and useful.

You'll come across more than a few words that are new to you. Unlike too many books addressed to young people, this one isn't going to stoop to conquer. Instead of speaking in the private teen lingo popular at this moment in time, this book employs language that will be operative when it's time to hand it to your kids. Anyway, how're you going to expand your vocabulary and stretch your mind if you don't ever confront something new? (In most cases you won't even have to look up the words as they'll be surrounded with contextual words with which you're familiar.)

While this is a manual, it's not a workbook. The object of these paragraphs is to help you ENJOY this life to the fullest. There is no higher or better use of human existence. For when joy is lacking, so is compassion, pride, and freedom. Nothing will satisfy a person incapable of enJOYment, and joyless people are inclined to interfere with their neighbors joys.

No skipping

The first part of this book is stacked with stuff that makes what follows lots more meaningful. So don't go rushing ahead to the "S-E-X" chapter until you've opened your mind to the previous bits on *responsibility* and *opposites* and the *two realities*, etc. Like the song sez, "...the beginning is a very good place to start." That way you at least know when you've reached the end.

Additional Editions

The first edition of this book was sponsored by The Centers For Teenage Discovery as a review of experiences that came up in the Centers' self-discovery workshops. But it soon became apparent that the book should have a life of its own as it would touch more lives and serve more people than the workshops ever could (being limited by time, place, and money). So a second edition was published for national distribution, followed by a subsequent edition and numerous reprintings and now this: a grand new, expanded edition which confronts matters of the moment: AIDS, the kamikaze behavior of contemporary teens, melting polar ice caps and other exciting, real-world stuff.

Word Play

The success this book has enjoyed to date should tell the publisher to "leave well enough alone...don't fix what works!" Good advice, but it is only human to wish to improve on the past. Words are weird devices – they mean different things at different times to different people. Words are like a blob of damp clay – so full of possibilities, so hard to keep hands off; especially when those words deal with the art of living: how to keep your head screwed on right.

Making a bookful of words appealing and meaningful to you is no easy task. It's not a question of intelligence. It's a matter of interest. Keeping a 16-year-old interested in the printed word requires some pretty zingy stuff. It also means resisting the temptation to write what the PTA, the FBI, the board of education, and U2 think is appropriate. You get plenty of that already!

Why?

It is fair to ask why this modest manual has been cheered by teenagers, saluted by parents, applauded by educators and other concerned professionals. What's in it that isn't to be found in other books about the greening years?

Well, the first thing to know is that bless'd few books about the teen years are written for teens! Apparently, publishers subscribe to the conventional wisdom that teenagers can't or won't read what some adult has to say about their experience.

The second thing to know is what little there is to read about the threshold years concentrates on the world of form and function without acknowledging the inner realms of being and feeling. Here again is the adult assumption that teenagers wouldn't be interested in worlds of their own making. C'mon folks, where were you when the flower children planted diamonds in the sky (whose blossoms we're still harvesting)?

1

Seven Years
of Heaven and Hell

You are at the point where any future can overtake you.

The library is packed with learned books about every stage of growing up. And each phase is said to be critical, some kind of crisis or Moment of Truth.

Well, there are moments, and there are moments! But the present moment is probably as momentous as any you'll experience; at least until you reach the flipside of the teenage years, the frantic fifties, when your body starts folding instead of blooming.

So it's not just your imagination – a lot of stuff is happening to you these days that has never happened before and will never happen again. For some of you it's confusing, frustrating, maybe emotionally painful. For others it's just great, a super good time. One thing the teen years are *not*, not for anyone, are boring.

The fact that the teenage period is an upper for some and a double downer for others serves to introduce one of life's great mysteries. How come? Why does everything good seem to happen to some people while a black cloud shadows others? One thing's for sure – it has nothing to do with luck. You can't isolate any single cause of one person's downfall or another's success – why Joan's a genius and Dick's a dummy, how come Tom survived the ghetto while Sally became a teenage prostitute. A personality is an evolving ecological system (that affects the whole universe and is, in turn, affected by it).

"Every minute you are a full statement of your being." You're always the sum total of your past up to the present. So there's no denying your past, no way to wipe it out. But that's no reason to walk backwards through life focused on what has passed. The way to avoid pitfalls and surmount hurdles is to face them.

Many believe the past is not just the remembered past but includes past incarnations; past lives if you prefer. You did not spring out of nothingness. It's bad logic as well as bad physics to think nothing can become something. (Neither can something become nothing!)

Your consciousness has stored every impression since it became conscious. This memory bank generates inclinations, attitudes, aptitudes, and tendencies. You tend to be a certain kind of person. Also contributing to your tendencies is environment: the sum total of social, economic, educational, political, cultural, even climatic conditions and heredity. The ingenious gene arranges the physical facts of your life.

It is worthless to wonder which of the three parts of our past – heredity, environment, consciousness – has the most impact on your present. What is, *is*. The only question to ask is – what are you doing with what is?

The past is powerful, but you are not its pawn, you are not powerless over it. That energizing force called willpower is capable of rising above or transcending the past.

To say 'bad blood' or a 'bad neighborhood' determines the outcome of one's life is a cop-out. You can make your life come out any way you wish. People don't want to know this. It puts the monkey on their back!

We love to consider ourselves victims of forces beyond our control. That's hogwash. This doesn't mean various people don't have real limitations, but those handicaps have more to do with your physical package than the 'real' you, the Inspector, the consciousness that witnesses the physical world. So a one-legged person would be foolish to wish to be an Olympic highjumper, and wise to concentrate on chess. But that is not the point of this chapter.

While it is never too early, and never too late to get your act together, a person just doesn't have all the necessary equipment or the motivation before 14 or 15. As a general rule, your body is going through such dramatic changes prior to 14 that it is asking too much of an adolescent to do anything more than keep two feet on the ground.

Changing from a caterpillar to a butterfly is quite enough without expecting he/she to understand what's going on. Twelve to 14 is a hanging-in-there period. But come 15, you're ready to fly; physically ready. The fact that so many of you suffer broken wings indicates there's more to flying than equipment. There's overcoming fear, developing confidence, technique. But that's still not the point of this chapter.

The point is this: between 15 and 18 comes the first opportunity to decide how you want your life to be. At 15 you've got the body and basic smarts to get your act together.

There's no equivalent to those three momentous years. People are 'young adults' for a good ten years (depending on who's doing the counting). And you'll be an adult for twenty to thirty years. And an old adult for another twenty or so years. Fifteen to 18 is just a tick of time compared to those upcoming periods. And yet, within these brief teenage years, such a lot of stuff comes down on you: sex, higher education, financial independence, career choices, lifestyle options, maybe even love.

Fifteen to 18 is a crash course in lifemanship. Think of all the new sensations, realizations, experiences that occur in that short span. (Adults have been known to go twenty years without coming up against anything new!) And for the first time you're facing the full force of society's prohibitions (all the 'do nots') and expectations (all those 'dos'). How about that – just when you're ready to soar, life comes along and burdens you with all that baggage. That's life! What a downer. Doesn't seem fair, does it? Well, it is – as you will see in an upcoming chapter.

Because the teen years are such a brief encounter, the adult world is inclined to look the other way. That's why teenagers are isolated; why there's so little literature written *for* teenagers (and why none of it is written *by* teenagers), why so few organizations exist to represent you, why teenagers have no clout, no authority, no 'rights.' There's just no time to get organized. The 16-year-old who decides to make a case for teenage 'rights' will be 21 before anyone listens. Then he/she is no longer interested.

But for all the apparent problems that are unique to these three tumultous years, there are some unique advantages, golden opportunities which will never again occur. Number One among these is the opportunity to be *your self*.

Notes to Myself

Notes to Myself

2

Getting Your Act Together

"If you are to get out of prison, the first thing you must realize is: you are in prison! If you think you are free, you can't escape."

—GURDJIEFF

"Be yourself." When someone says that, they usually mean, "Stop acting, quit pretending...be real."

Being real should be the easiest of all things to be. You shouldn't have to work at being real. You shouldn't have to study how to be real, or have to spend time in front of a mirror deciding who the real you is. And yet, most of us have a difficult time being what we are, teenagers as well as adults. You are so busy being a student, a football hero, a lover, a trouble-maker, or a tomboy that you're left with no time or place to be whatever it is that's behind those masks.

Very early in life we are handed scripts and are expected to act accordingly. We go through all these acts without ever getting in touch with who's doing the acting. That's a trap, a jail without walls. Most people remain prisoners to their acts without knowing it – without knowing how easy (and essential) it is to be free.

It is impossible for a doctor to develop any self-confidence if he thinks that he is a doctor! He'll be confident of his doctoring abilities, but that's not *self*-confidence. There's nothing wrong with being a doctor or a piano player or a homemaker or a congressman. That's what bodies and minds do. But you are more than a body and a mind. If you don't think so, why do you call it *your* body, *your* mind...how come you can lose a finger or all four limbs and still be *you?*

What is critically important is that you realize the difference between you and the roles you play. What a difference that makes. It provides you with an anchor to hold you steady in stormy times. You'll never need to sing that sad song, "Is That All There Is?" When you know that your roles are not you, that they are just what the external you (the ego!) is doing – what 'goeswith' you – then you can handle the ups or downs that come with playing doctor or housewife or singer or burglar or lover or president or teenager. That allows your consciousness to watch and witness what is happening to your physical parts and ego.

When you can separate your self from your roles, then you are the actor and the director. That puts you in complete charge

of the whole production. You can continue in your roles better
able to accept what happens to the character you are playing. If
things get too heavy, you The Director can step in and change the
scenery, the script, the interpretation. Try it. It's easy.

When you wake up to a face full of zits (which will make
difficult your role as the most-beautiful-girl-in-the-sophomore
class), realize that what is happening to your face is zits. *You* are
not zits. Your face has them. That doesn't make them go away. If
pimples are a problem, you've got a problem. If all you are is a
beautiful girl, then you are no more! Your life is ruined. But if you
can witness you having this problem and say "Oh, dear – what's
happening to me right now is a lousy complexion," then you've
separated your consciousness from what's happening to your face.
That puts you in the driver's seat. You are no longer a victim,
being taken for a ride by forces beyond your control.

Of course, most people – whether 15 or 50 – think they
know who they are. They'll recite a list of titles or attributes –
goeswith things like "I am a man: a tall, dark, handsome fellow
who's an architect and a Republican." They will also tell you what
they want to be: a millionaire, an oceanographer, an actress, a
mother, etc., etc.

You are not a teenager any more than your mother is a
mother or your father is a father. Those are what you do, roles you

choose to play. But when you think that's all you are, that will be all you are. And none of those roles is enough. Otherwise, doctors, housewives, physicists, etc., wouldn't be going to psychiatrists to find their *selves*.

We've spent a lot of time on examples of what happens when you don't have a handle on who you really are as opposed to who you appear to be. The advantage of knowing there's something more to you than the roles you play is that it produces *self-*confidence: a very good thing to have. People who lack *self-*confidence are always trying to prove themselves to others. And the ways they try to prove themselves is to get control of others' egos – through wealth, physical or political power, with tears, laughs, etc., etc., etc.

The person who knows who he/she is and has come to terms with that reality is not all wrapped up in him/herself, not constantly trying to prove something, not always feeling threatened and poorly treated. They don't have to be concerned about what other people think of them.

It is the rare person who is not concerned with impressing. You can't be you while trying to impress somebody else. You can't really hear what somebody else is saying if you're thinking about what they are thinking of you. Even if your method of impressing is being a 'good listener,' it's superficial listening. It's listening with an ulterior motive. When somebody knows who he/she is, he/she is able to concentrate on others, rather than what will impress others. That is what really impresses other people, being totally interested in them. You can only do that when you aren't concerned about your own status. Until you come to terms with yourself, you're going to have problems relating to others.

Being confident of one's ability to be a lawyer or a highjumper or a boxer is fine but it's a far cry from having *self-*confidence. You're only a lawyer, a jumper, etc., part-time. That doesn't give you the confidence to be a good father or fisherman or whatever else you do.

You've probably heard your mom complain about "having no time to be me." What she's really saying is, "Who am I?" That's what's behind the rush to discover 'me' via conciousness-expanding movements. People are at last getting wise to the realization that they will always feel inadequate and threatened and off-center until they have a focus, a ballast, a *self* to be. There's no *self-*identity to being a mother or a millionaire. Those are titles.

What you are transcends any time or place or society or title. *You are realizations.* To be sure, you are also sensations, emotions, thumbs, brains, nerves. But those are your media, the equipment your consciousness employs to express itself on the physical plane. Realizations are manifestations of pure or super conciousness. They are insight; private inner experiences that are dependent on no outside cause. This essential, inner you can function independent of the outer you; that is, it needs no body to realize itself. If you'd like to experience this state of no-mind without fooling with psychedelics or spending months chanting in a Tibetan cave – struggle into a wet suit, suspend yourself in a tank of body-temp water, breathing through a mouthpiece. Cover the eyes so no light can touch them, and the ears so no sound reaches them. When your senses have nothing to sense you experience an incredible ecstasy. Total completeness, total togetherness, total security, total desirelessness. For those moments you are pure consciousness detached from your mortal coil. The realizations that come to you in this state are not generated by physical stimulus, nor do they start in your brain/intellect. They must pass through that system, your bodyworks, but they don't start there. Returning to the world of weights and measures, sounds, smells, tastes and feels – you will realize how that body of yours only makes things difficult, gross, confusing. But most of all you would realize that the body is baggage (however necessary it is for this trip), that you can and will continue to be you without it. A rather sensational piece of information.

A preacherman would no doubt say 'soul' is the purest essence, but let's not get hung up with words. It's your 'center' place…it's no place and every place. It's the Big Mystery. But it's no mystery how to use this source of All.

Notes to Myself

3

The Two Realities

"There are more things in heaven and earth, Horatio,
Than are dreamt of in your philosophy." —William Shakespeare

Everyone operates in two 'worlds,' within two realities.
(Most people don't know it, but that doesn't change what is!)
There's the dense world of material realities. And the space-y
world that is more difficult for you to witness. Included in this
difficult-to-see world are things like energy vibrations that carry
light and sound.

Even if you acknowledge the presence of both, it's really
difficult to keep these two realities straight. That's because we operate in both worlds simultaneously. Our conscious self is of one;
our physical self of the other. For most people, only the seeable,
touchable, hearable, tastable, smellable is real. So we are constantly being confused by 'mysterious,' unseen happenings.

It is *trés* tricky coping with the two realities; keeping them in balance. One is always trying to dominate the other. So people tend to be super physical or totally immersed in the metaphysical. (That's why mystics are usually to be found far removed from cities…and why they are surrounded by devotees who feed them and shoo away the tigers and vipers.)

The so-called material world, the world bounded by your five senses, let us name that 'Reality I.' Here's where things are hot and cold, heavy and hurtful. It's when you can tune-out the low frequencies that radiate from material objects and tune-in to higher vibrational levels – the consciousness level – that things get interesting. This is the phenomenal world of so-called miracles; where the impossible becomes possible. Let us call that, 'Reality II,' where you get to create your own experiences un-bounded by physical limitations.

The higher consciousness (what Freud called 'superego') can motivate the body to outdo itself, produce a 'peak performance.' The consciousness can do even more amazing things when it detaches from the body: it can travel in time and space, among other things. And just because the scientific establishment can't get a fix on this phenomena doesn't mean it doesn't happen! It simply means it's beyond science.

You see, all our reference points are relative to the material or physical plane; that is, Reality I. When we talk about something being impossible (like ESP, out of the body experiences, clairvoyance, and other psychic phenomena), we're referring to what is observable to our gross sense of sight, touch, smell, etc. Walking through a brick wall is, in fact, impossible relative to our material bodies. However, our awareness or consciousness can pass through that wall to experience what's on the other side, to communicate with what's there.

The confusion produced by these two Realities, I and II, has produced some legendary misunderstandings. Like the Sermon on the Mount: Jesus was directing that lecture to some pretty enlightened souls, his Disciples. So he was speaking to an elevated consciousness operating on the Reality II level. But Jesus' advice got carried down the mountain side to the world of Reality I, where its application has caused all kinds of mischief. The Hindus have a parable about this this sort of thing:

There was once a holy man who came to a village. The villagers warned him that he must not go along a certain road because a venomous snake which had killed many people always lay there. "It won't hurt me," said the holy man, and continued on. Sure enough, the snake approached, reared its head, hissing and ready to strike; but when it saw the holy man it prostrated humbly at his feet. The sage taught it to give up the idea of biting and killing. Following instructions, the snake, having received initiation into spiritual life with a sacred name of God, crawled off to its hole to pray and meditate; and the holy man proceeded on his way. Soon the boys of the village discovered the change in the character of the snake. Knowing that it was now harmless, they would attack it with sticks and stones whenever it came out of its hole – but the snake would never strike back. After a while the snake grew so weak from its injuries that it would scarcely crawl. Only rarely at night it would come out of its hole in search of food.

When next the holy man came to that village, he was told that the snake was dead. "That's impossible," said the sage. "It cannot die until it has attained the fruit of the holy word with which it was initiated." He went to the snake's hole and called it. Hearing its teacher's voice, the snake came squirming out, crippled from the blows it had received and terribly thin because it was not getting enough to eat. The holy man questioned it about the reason for its condition. "Revered sir," the snake replied, "you asked me not to harm any creature. I have been living on leaves and fruit. Perhaps that's why I am so thin." The snake had developed the virtue of forgiveness and had forgotten the boys had almost killed it. The sage said: "No, there must be a reason other than want of food that is responsible for your condition. Try to remember." Then the snake recalled: "Oh yes, some village boys beat me, but I wouldn't bite them. I just lay silently and suffered their torments," The snake expected to be praised for resisting evil. To its great surprise, however, the holy man became quite cross: "How foolish you are," he cried. "I told you not to bite. Did I tell you not to hiss?"

So if you are operating on the material level, as you are, you must contend with sticks and stones. You've got to know when to 'hiss' and when to turn the other cheek.

Hissing should be the next to last resort, before striking out. If you know when and how to hiss, you may never have to strike! Once violence is resorted to, whether defensive or not, you lose. People who fight have been defeated before the first blow is struck. They have lost their humanity, retreated to their animal past. Hissing is somewhere in-between. It's a way of saying, "Watch it – I'm capable of being a viper; don't mess with me." It is much better to threaten than to act. That's why peace-loving nations arm themselves: to keep the peace.

Before hissing, try smiling. A smile can be very disarming. Not a thin, little nervous smile, but a great big open confident smile that says, "I'm okay, you're okay." It's really hard to be suspicious of or mad at someone who is smiling (as long as the smile isn't a smartass smirk).

Getting along in this me-against-you Reality I world is real simple if you're a one-dimensional type who sees life as a simple matter of good/bad, black/white, win/lose. This type of person considers life a great big contest: capitalism versus communism, Christians versus pagans, North versus South, our school versus your school, America versus Japan, rich versus poor, Us versus Them. Power is the sole obsession of this sort. It's a hangover from our Hunter ancestors (when "kill or be killed" was the law – jungle version). There's a little Tarzan in us all. But too many of us act like apemen every waking hour. They are closer to man's past than man's future.

It is less simple to make it in this Reality I world when you recognize there is another reality. The two seem to pull in opposite directions. The public or ego-you seeks pleasure in physical form: eating, drinking, sex, applause, winning. The private or inner-you seeks higher, less physical forms of pleasure – what we call 'inspirational' pleasures: music, religion, literature, doing a kindness.

Most people only have a faint acquaintance with their higher conciousness, so the lower ego-consciousness usually dominates and they spend most of their lives acting like Ivan the Terrible. That faint little inner voice peeps through on Sundays and at Christmastime, when you're alone, and especially before sleep (if you don't go to bed with the radio dominating your consciousness!).

Because what you do is often in conflict with how you feel, you accumulate a lot of guilt. Some people get rid of it in a confessional manner – private, ritualistic or psychiatric. Some of us solve the conflict by shutting off the conscience, that inner voice. They surround themselves with TV, radio, drugs, booze, sex, fighting, sports – never giving the inner voice a chance to be heard. Pity.

Reality I and II need not be in conflict. Being a moral, compassionate, tolerant, joyful person doesn't doom you to failure. A pretty good definition of a 'together' person is one who keeps both Realities working together synergistically. Those are the people who seem to "have everything"; they're good sports, good fun, good students, everything comes their way, everything works, their life works! It's as if they had an extra power source, two engines instead of one...which is about it! Reality II can make Reality I better. It isn't just somewhere to hide from the material world – it sharpens the tools you dig with, stimulates peak performance. The idea is to apply Reality II *principles* to Reality I *practices*, like applying so-called Christian principles ("Do Unto Others...") in business dealings. It pays. Feels good, too. Also, it's

a lot easier to overcome fears of failure, an unpleasant environment, a lousy school, cruddy clothes, a funny nose if you know
you are of the cosmos.

Still, nobody's perfect at juggling the two Realities; even
Jesus had a few bobbles. When that happens, don't quit. Pick up
and start again. Practice makes perfect. That's what you're doing
now – practicing.

Notes to Myself

Notes to Myself

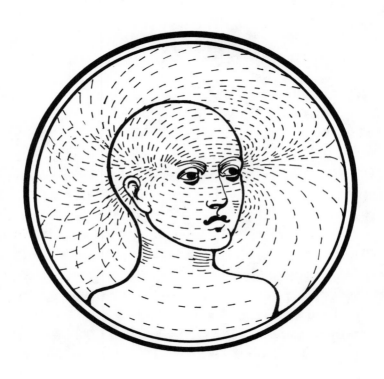

4

How Do You Know
You Know?

Stop talking, stop thinking and there is nothing you will not understand.

There's only one way to *know* something; that's to experience it.

Somebody can tell you why it's impossible to walk through a wall, and you may accept their reasons without experiencing a flat nose. But when you take somebody's word for anything, you don't *really* know. You're just accepting, agreeing. We obviously can't seek first-hand experience about everything. We've got to take somebody's word for lots of things. If Boeing's chief test tilot says the plane will fly, we are inclined to accept that and buy a ticket.

'Knowing' that comes by means of agreement is what you call 'knowledge.' Knowing that results from personal experience is the basis of wisdom. So a knowledgeable man is not necessarily a wise man.

We get most of our knowledge about ourselves from other people from the way they experience us. If the teacher says you're dumb, you figure you must be because teachers are smart. So you play the dummy role. If you never spend any time experiencing yourself, then all you'll ever know about yourself is what you see mirrored in other people's desires and fears. You become a reflection of these second-hand perceptions.

Well, we've already established that the face you show to others has little to do with the feelings that operate behind that face. It's as if you went out dressed in a monkey suit and got yourself locked up in a zoo. If all you are is what other people see then you're stuck with your act. If we shed our monkey suits – or however you dress your ego – we come face to face with what's inside. To do this consciously, without resorting to such things as psychedelic chemicals† requires withdrawing from the external realities – as in meditation. You've got to get your body and ego out of the way. The objective is to stop thinking about you and all the things that affect you. The idea is to vacuum your head *to quiet the mind* which involves getting out of your mind; that is, your rational intellect.

---

†Psychedelics can be a shortcut to experiencing who or what we are. Nobody who has ever used psychedelics thinks all they are is a physical package. Of course, to suddenly, without any preparation, experience that your consciousness can operate apart from your fleshly facade can be quite a shock. That's why psychedelics are nothing to play around with. There are safer, more righteous ways of experiencing your source.

The Western world resists things like meditation because, according to our values, to stop thinking is to stop functioning. 'Thinking' is our pride and joy (though, in fact, it is the source of all our miseries). Shutting down the cerebral cortex (the thinking generator in the brain) is related to going out of our minds. That's where you must go to get to the higher levels of truth. There are all kinds of techniques for developing this ability. They take time and effort.

It is probably asking too much of a teenager to retreat from the physical reality once or twice a day...to be quiet and still, to stop participating in the world of objects, and spend some private minutes in Reality II. But it is worthwhile to learn how and why it's done, so that in later life you know how to shut out the insanity of the material world and recharge your batteries by plugging directly into the cosmic power source.

Meditation, or just plain daydreaming is very beneficial, but that doesn't mean you must do it or else. If you aren't curious, if you don't feel any great need or desire to switch off Reality I and let yourself float in Reality II – forget it. If you don't have the motivation, it will never happen anyway. And for most people, the motivation comes late(r) in life when the head is cluttered with crap – fears, anxieties, disappointments, resentments. That's when the need to debug yourself becomes a necessity, else the mind becomes so burdened it may break down or blow a fuse (which is an approximate description of a nervous breakdown: Nature's way of making you switch off Reality I). Anyone who can experience the state of no-thing early in life will never need Nature's shock treatment or the ministrations of cults and gurus.

And in case you've lost track of the connection between meditation and this chapter's heading – the link is this: You'll never really *know* anything until you know the knower is not the brain. And if it isn't the brain (the microprocessor of your computer system), it must be the consciousness (that which programs your computer system's operational software). Just because we can't locate the consciousness with a scalpel doesn't mean it isn't there! One hundred years ago we couldn't locate X-rays, much less radio waves – but they were 'there' nonetheless, waiting to be recognized and utilized.

Don't get the idea that just because Reality II is a higher, non-mortal level of conscious experience you should excuse yourself from Reality I, by whatever means. No, no, no, no, NO! We are not here to deny we are here. So forget about hiding behind a smokescreen of dope and violence or applause or any of the other stuff that keeps you unconscious. People who drop out aren't getting out. It's no way to escape. It's a deadend – meaning you'll have to return to 'Go' sooner or later.

The only reason you should know about the knower, the consciousness, is because it helps you operate in the so-called 'real' world of Reality I. It helps you soar like an eagle over the badlands below. Knowing that the knower, the private inner you, is tied to the eternal cosmos gives you a lift, raises you above the ego traps of drugs, violence, wealth, resentment. You can only be free when you are not dependent on physical attachments. Knowing that is half the battle. Doing something about it is the other half.

Notes to Myself

5

Opposites

We try to be pendulums that swing to only one side.

You can't be wealthy unless someone is poor, you can't know beauty without seeing ugliness. Light requires dark to be seen, as objects require space to be perceived as solids. Birth is inconceivable without death, as is summer without winter. Evil exists for the sake of Good and vice versa. Every coin has its reverse side, every 'plus' must be balanced by a 'minus,' and *every* action produces an opposite reaction. That's really all there is to the so-called 'facts of life.' All else flows therefrom: masculine/feminine, young/old, meek/bold, winners/losers. There could be no sadists without masochists. No doves without hawks. No yin without its yang. Imagine a world where everyone is beautiful, everyone rich. How would you know who is rich? How would you know there's such a thing as rich? Losers, ugliness, evil all serve to make their opposites possible.

This is not a lot of obscure fluff. Opposites or duality is the law of the universe. This is something worth thinking about. When you come to realize losers fulfill a necessary function (they make winners possible!), that some people are attractive because others are unattractive, then you will never be confused by 'bad' things in a perfect universe created by a loving God.† How could you conceive of God as perfect if He did not allow you to know imperfection for purposes of contrast. It makes no difference if you substitute 'Nature' for 'God,' or a 'Greater Power,' or the 'Great White Light.'

Whatever you call the original creative force, the source of all energy, it created a perfectly balanced universe. The balance is a product of equal and opposite extremes. The rhythm of life is created by ups and downs, highs and lows. Everyone has both. There is nothing to do with this rhythm except to just realize it. It is what accounts for our inconsistencies. Despite being surrounded by evidence to the contrary, we expect people to be consistent and average; to always be kind or always mean. We actually become irritated when someone whom we love to hate does something nice. Either we don't believe it or we resent it, "How dare you act nice after being hateful for so long. What are you trying to do, confuse me, just to be mean?"

---

†"I am Lord, not of light alone, but of darkness also… I the Lord destroy with darkness. But with darkness, I also create. The wise discern this. Fools, deluded by outward appearance create a web of their follies." – Book of Tokens

It is all too possible for a clergyman to mount the pulpit and inspire his flock with great spiritual wisdom and the next day be arrested for lewd conduct. What's disquieting about that bit of news isn't lewdness *per se*, but that it was a minister being lewd! People can't handle such opposites as 'lewdity' *and* 'minister.' So either we just won't believe he was exposing himself or we reject his ability to preach. We become very uninspired about his sermon last Sunday, which is dumb. Why throw the baby out with the wash? We reject a good side when a bad side shows itself. That's when we should be charitable, balance the good against the bad – not go to the extremes that happen when you ignore one side and concentrate on the other. Life doesn't work like that, so why should you?

Life is a constantly unfolding, ongoing process involving the entire (unimaginable) universe. We only see people and events in the perspective of our tick of time. And so it may appear that crime sometimes pays, that tyrants often triumph and all manner of wrongdoing goes unpunished. That's because we rush to judgement. We expect to see 'right' prevail here and now, while we're watching. This is wandering a bit from the 'rule of opposites,' but as long as we're off course for the moment, let's continue the detour long enough to note that our system of temporal justice is represented by counter-balanced scales – the purpose of which is equality. But that kind of balance is more theoretical than actual;

more manmade than real.† Perfect justice or balance is delivered on the cosmic or Reality II level. In the world of form and function, bodies and intellects are created unequal. People do suffer injustice in Reality I.

Minorities in America have, in fact, been culturally subjected by a white-dominated society. But the soul, or spirit, or consciousness of these men and women will find justice on the level where there is no whiteness or blackness. Here and now, however, the scales are always tipped to one or another extreme. The fact that we try to right the imbalance by law and moral persuasion is testimony to man's divine spirit and increasing moral nature. It is one of many characteristics that separates *Homo sapiens* from other life forms. Dogs and fish and plants show little or no concern for their less fortunate brethren. Only man (and perhaps some mammals) demonstrates compassion, the ability to put yourself into somebody else's space – to feel what they feel as if you were linked (which, of course, you are!).

The rule of opposites is also what causes us to covet the things we don't have. For in order to get something, you must first lack something. The person who lacks wealth desires money. Ca-

---

†In the same fashion that 'averages' are unreal. For instance, we always talk about average rainfall, but there is seldom if ever a winter when it rains no more or less than 'average.' It takes a lot of very wet and very dry winters to establish a meaningful average; just as it requires many extremely different people to produce an average person (that non-person you are always being compared to!).

reer women want families and housewives want independence.
The sailor dreams of settling down while the farmer wants to put
the wind to his back. (More about this follows in the chapter en-
titled "Problems.") The lesson here is that you can't have and eat
that well-known cake! You can't be faster unless someone is
slower. You can't become full without having been empty. You
won't feel joy without knowing sadness. This doesn't mean you're
supposed to like the downside. It just means there are two sides to
everything (on the Reality I level).

It should be recognized, also, that Reality I does not hand
out an equal number of 'goods' and 'bads.' As mentioned above,
some people appear to suffer more bad than good. An Untouch-
able in Calcutta knows only hunger, illness, hopelessness. Or so it
would seem from our point of view. But the rule of opposites is a
relative measure. When you are very low it doesn't take much of a
lift to make you feel high. When you are starving, a crust makes a
banquet. A child who has never had (nor seen) a toy can be made
happy with a stick and a stone. This view may strike you as being
a bit heartless. The example is not meant to justify a diet of crusts.
Why that is one man's fate and not another's is another discussion. The point being made is that 'bad' on your scale might be
'good' on somebody else's. Some people experience poorness on
an annual income of $50,000, whereas $5,000 is rich to another.
Neither can imagine how the other is possible.

6

Responsibility and Irresponsibility

If you 'get' this chapter, you can close the book and go about your
business because you will have all you need to make the most of your
teenage years…or any years.

The person who takes responsibility for his/her own
thoughts and deeds is the person who will never suffer resentments…the worst disease *Homo sapiens* can contract. It is the one
psychological ailment from which there is no recovery…except by
taking responsibility.

Most of the things that happen to us happen as a result of
some easily remembered action or attitude. When Jeff, a linebacker on his school's football team, gets a tooth knocked out
because of a flying tackle, he doesn't (or shouldn't) blame his lost
tooth on the runner's shoe. Whether Jeff thought about it or not,
when he decided to fly through the air he was risking a broken

tooth. That doesn't make his lost tooth 'good' or 'bad,' it just makes it his responsibility. But look what happens when that linebacker feels a need to blame his lost tooth on the runner. One, he's lost a tooth. Two, he's gained a resentment. The broken tooth can be fixed. But all that venom resentment generates won't go away so easily. If the self-appointed 'victim' meets the object of his resentment in a parking lot after the game and asks impolitely why he kicked his tooth out, the other player isn't going to agree. He's going to say, "You're crazy, man. You tackled me." Just what Mr Toothless expected. The rat denied everything. That just hardens the linebacker's resentment

Now Jeff is working on hating that runner, and little by little he's beginning to hate himself by that much. He's contracted a disease that can only get worse – until he takes responsibility for his own actions. All he has to do is realize who did what. Admit it to himself. That's all it takes. That unravels what has become a complicated problem and makes it disappear. All the linebacker's left with is some dental work and another experience. He doesn't carry the burden of resentment into all his other affairs.

Another situation: Bridget, 15, goes out to study with a friend on a school night. She agrees to be home no later than 11 o'clock. Some boys drop by her friend's while she's there and they decide to make a Big Mac run. One thing leads to another, it gets to be eleven, but Bridget doesn't want to be a wet blanket. When they finally pull up in front of her house, it's quarter to twelve. Her mom spots the car and the boys, leaps to conclusions and jumps all over Bridget who, of course, feels she did everything reasonable to get home on time; and in any event, she certainly did nothing wrong. So Miss Prissy's reaction is to slam her bedroom door in mother's face – which makes an already angry mother more so. So she gets father, who, through clenched teeth, tells Bridget she's not to set foot out of the house for one month. Bridget screams, "I hate you. You're awful," and the next few days are miserable for everyone.

Wouldn't it have been easier for Bridget to allow she was late and regret it? It *was* her responsibility, whatever the difficulties. And it was her decision to go along to Mc Donald's however harmless and reasonable that was. Had she reacted to her mom's over-reaction with that opening acknowledgement, mother would have calmed down, listened to the ensuing story and in the end sympathized with Bridget. After a for-the-record, "Don't do that again," her parents would have walked away from the matter and everyone could have gone to bed wearing a smile. No lies, no resentments, no personal compromises or giving in.

Taking responsibility for whatever happens to you is right simply because it makes your life work better – the only valid reason for doing anything.

Sometimes it isn't so clear where you went 'wrong.' A lot of un-good things happen that don't appear to be traceable to any act or attitude on your part. Well, too often that's your ego's defense mechanism working to protect itself. Most times, if you hunt hard enough, you'll discover you created the cause that produced the effect – however delayed it was in manifesting itself.

Some thinkers perceive of tragedy (ill fate befalls the seemingly innocent) as a harvesting of acts committed in a previous existence. Your karma. But most often, you don't have to go back that far. Maybe beyond last week. Maybe as far back as childhood. But somewhere back there is the seed of what has been harvested.

That's how the universe works: with perfect consistency. That's the only way it can work. If anything were off-kilter (like a cause producing no effect or an action producing no reaction), the whole universe would go 'tilt' and self-destruct. The fact that it hasn't indicates that everything is still in perfect working order. Maybe *you* have decided not to like what's happening to your body and ego. That's *your* decision, and *your* responsibility. But the universe keeps working whether or not it's to *your* liking.

The two parts that make the universe work are cause and effect. You can't have one without the other. Effects don't always have an identifiable cause, but that doesn't mean there isn't one.

It just means you can't or won't comprehend it. In that case accept it. When something goes amiss in your life, accept at face value that you are the cause of it. One: it's true. Two: you escape all those personally disturbing feelings that come from blaming it on parents, teachers, coach, boyfriend, the Republicans, the Devil, Fate, the weather, ad nauseam.

People who hang on to what they judge to be injustices are crippled by them. *"How could they have done that to me...,"* *"What did I ever do to deserve that?"* *"I was quietly minding my own business when this big pig of a cop..."* No doubt about it, big cops have been known to walk up to innocent bystanders at a friendly neighborhood riot and thump them smartly on the head. And that bystander would be sympathized with after his release from the emergency ward, if he felt he had suffered unjust treatment.

But the universe doesn't assign such labels as 'unjust' or 'innocent' to people or events. In order to be knocked on the noggin, you had to be in the vicinity of noggin-knocking. That was *your* choice. It was a choice that involved risk. (Every choice does!) Even if you couldn't help but be in the middle of the SWAT-team offensive – you were, in fact, there. And there's where you should leave it. But most of us make matters worse by picking up the burden of resentment. The hate for that cop carries to all cops. One more monkey to carry around on your back for the rest of your life. Who needs it. Just say, "Oops! I was there. Turned out to be the wrong place to be." Then the worst is over. You've got a sore head. You've been inconvenienced. But you haven't been crippled with hate. This is not being a doormat. Nobody's recommending you roll over and play dead.

When Jesus advised, "Turn the other cheek..." he wasn't being holier-than-thou. He was being, as usual, terribly practical. To "suffer the slings and arrows of outrageous fortune" is indeed ennobling. But to "set up arms against a sea of troubles" will surely cause worse troubles.

Human beings cry out for justice; and it is there. The universe, God, call it what you will, metes out perfect justice. You don't have to play judge. Trust the atom and the galaxies to serve you properly. If you choose to head up river without a paddle, don't blame the river for making it tough.

Nobody suffers self-pity like teenagers. If it's any consolation, it would *appear* that you are the victim of forces beyond your control. Somebody else does appear to physically run your life. You are burdened with expectations you didn't ask for. But don't get suckered in. You'll pay a price for blaming your lot on anyone else but yourself.

'Blame' is, of course, a value judgement that you'd be better off not to make. When you blame somebody or something, you are in effect saying that you're helpless; a victim of circumstances beyond your control because you cannot change 'them' or 'it.' If you've got a gun maybe you can control somebody's physical movements, but not their spirit – not their thoughts and feelings.

On the other hand, when you take personal responsibility for something you've judged 'bad,' then you are in a position to make it right. *Only you can do something about you.* That's all you can do. That's all you need to do. (If each and every person cleaned up his or her own act, nobody would be messed up…it'd be heaven on Earth.)

So jealousy, self-pity, resentment, injustice, and tragedy are cop-outs, ways to avoid the responsibility for running your own life.

As usual, it's easier to describe how something works in the negative than in the positive. But taking responsibility has its plus side – it's not just a way of reconciling or removing problems. Taking responsibility is also taking credit. When something good happens to you, it's no more good luck than bad things are bad luck. You are the cause of those good things. You deserve what you get. Even if you stumbled onto buried treasure while chasing butterflies. You were there. You made it happen. Enjoy.

7

Had Any Good Fantasies Lately?

"We are such stuff as dreams are made on."

—William Shakespeare

'Making Believe' is usually connected with daydreaming, and daydreaming is usually linked to *time-wasting,* the opposite of *doing* or *achieving.* And yet it is the act of 'making oneself believe anything is possible' that makes anything possible.

Dreaming of becoming a millionaire (a commonplace fantasy in America) is a necessary part of wanting to…which is essential to becoming. Making believe you are scaling Mt Everest is a necessary preliminary to *doing it.* It's the first part; what *goes with* creating the desire and acquiring the ability. Because you can in fact become a millionaire or a mountain climber; *the difference between wanting and becoming mostly is desire.*

The reason adults get into ruts is because adults stop making believe. That's because 1) they don't take the time, thinking it a waste of time, and 2) as people get older, their options are reduced; that is, a 40-year-old can't become an airline pilot or stewardess or a 39-year-old president, or a millionaire before 30, or an Olympic champion, etc. After 40, these 'can nots' become so numerous that they tend to obscure the 'can dos.' But the 17-year-old can be *anything* he wants to be. And making believe is part of making dreams come true.

There's a metaphysical principle involved here, called the Process of Affirmation, but there is no need to formalize a simple procedure. Just let your mind visualize the object of your desires. *Treat it like it has already happened.* If being a singer is your dream, dream of appearing before a sellout concert, or accepting a gold record. *See* yourself in recording sessions, being mobbed. Of course, when you dream of hit records, you've got to spend time developing the necessary skills. But as mentioned, daydreaming will generate doing-something-about-it. The concept has to precede the reality.

How this principle or process works is really not important. But, because our technological society teaches that understanding must preceed believing, let's see if words can describe the power of mind over matter.

First of all, you must realize that whatever it is you want to do can in fact be done by you; that is, you possess the potential for doing it. What prevents people from realizing their dreams or potential is appearances. Seeing an accomplished pianist flay his piano is apt to cause a non-player to think, "Wow, I could never do that." It's the thinking, of course, that actually does the preventing. Appearances trigger the thinking. Thinking you can't or won't plants a can't/won't chip in your memory bank, which your microprocessor is programmed to convert into actions. Over time, negative thoughts produce negative results. Successful thoughts generate successful results. It's as simple as that!

When it comes to physical prowess – things like skiing or tennis, for example – this kind of negative thinking prevents the body from doing what's right (what comes naturally). Thinking you can't, or thinking it's hard literally binds the muscles, screws up the coordination. You literally think yourself into a bind. But if instead of seeing yourself looking awkward and failing, you visualize yourself going through the serving or schussing motions enough times, when the time comes to act out your fantasy, your body will know what to do. It really will! It's been programmed with the right moves. Then it becomes just a matter of letting it happen, of not allowing the mind to interfere by sending the body failure instructions. You've got to believe you can do it not only beforehand but while you're doing it. That involves picturing the end result; where you want the ball to go rather than how to get it there, for instance. For if you were to break down a tennis serve into its component parts, you'd become hopelessly tangled in herky-jerky movements. It's enough to know what a proper service motion looks like, so you can see yourself looking like that. Picture the total effect, what you want to happen.

Granted, this is an oversimplification. You can't 'think' yourself into Wimbledon. Practice makes perfect. But you will much more quickly reach the point where results provide the incentive to practice. Most people don't take up diving or piano-playing or open-heart surgery because of the agony of becoming. But visualizing the ecstasy of being minimizes the agony of becoming. At the very least it's much, much easier to do anything if everyday you spend time seeing yourself doing it perfectly. Athletes and performers actually practice using their 'mind's eye.'

This Process of Affirmation can help you reach any goal, so long as it is specific enough to permit 'seeing' yourself doing it or getting it. It can help you win the affection of a certain girl or boy. It can help you get a certain car or house or job. Because if you make it happen in your mind, the physical reality will follow; you will begin doing the right things, being in the right places, associating with the right people that will lead to the right result. It's a matter of receptivity and self-confidence. Conditioning your mind

and body to make the necessary moves. The same way we condition ourselves to fear and fail.

It's much easier to do this at 15 than it is when so-called
'reality' makes daydreaming the last resort of fools. So leave yourself some time for this important pastime. Bedrooms and hilltops
are great places for daydreaming. And don't hesitate to surround
yourself with objects connected with your desires, such as posters
of Mt Everest, books about mountain climbing and that sort of
thing. It's using Reality II to control Reality I.

Notes to Myself

8

Why Parents Act That Way

"The reason children and their grandparents get along so well is that they have a common enemy!"

—Margaret Mead

Before your parents became parents, they didn't act that way. When your father goes to work, he doesn't act that way. When your mother is with friends, she doesn't act that way. The only time parents act like parents is when they are with you! Just as the only time you act like a son or a daughter is when your are with your mother and father.

Parents fuss and fume, snoop, spoil, nag, love and toil because that's how they perceive parents are supposed to behave.

Parents are people, and like most people they don't like being resisted. When fathers complain about kids' sloppy habits, your indifference to study, or the decibels your speakers are

putting out – he just wants to get said what he understands
fathers are supposed to say. He feels better having done what he
considers to be his job as a parent. He doesn't necessarily feel
good while he's doing it, but after it's over with, he feels better.
And that would be the end of it…if you'd merely accept the fact
he's doing his parent bit and say something like, "Yeah, I can
understand why you feel that way, Dad." That way he knows you
hear him. You have acknowledged his complaint…without
compromising yourself.

But instead of leaving it there, teenagers feel a need to defend themselves. Some do it with words, some with mumbles,
others with a sour, pained look. Well, dammit, all the old man
wanted was to have done with his father trip and move on to
something pleasant. But part of his idea of being a parent is to
take no smart-alecking from a know-nothing kid. So, he comes
back with threats…and away the both of you go, around and
around, getting nowhere except further apart.

Parents, at least most parents, don't enjoy hassles, nor do
they want to dominate. Being a tyrant is a full-time and
exhausting job.

Parents would prefer to spend their time enjoying themselves – and enjoying you enjoying yourself. Parents start acting

tyrannical when you oppose them or resist their efforts to execute the parental role; that is, telling you the 'right' thing to do. Opposition or resistance is what causes tension. Because society gives parents the right to tell you what to do, you are placed in the position of 'going along' or opposing. Of course, you don't see it that way. Because most parental advice is not what you want to hear you get the idea that they are against you.

There's an easy way to beg the question; to avoid the tension that results from opposition. It works like this: try placing your two index fingers tip-to-tip opposing each other, so they're pushing against each other. Neither gets anywhere. The result is wasted energy and frustration. Or, if one finger is stronger than the other then you have a 'winner' and 'loser.' Neither result is desirable. But if you raise one finger above the other and push, each goes its own way effortlessly. It works with people as well as with fingers. When you stand aside, you haven't retreated, you haven't compromised – you've just avoided an unnecessary, unpleasant confrontation. That's the end of it.

The point is this: parents are not 'wrong' to do what they do anymore than you are to be blamed for acting like a son or daughter. And you are not diminishing yourself by avoiding confrontations. You're just being wise – wiser than your parents were when they were in your shoes, most likely.

A few other points about parents. A mother and father have some not-to-be-denied advantages over their sons and daughters. First and foremost, every parent has been a teenager. Whereas blessed few teenagers have been parents! So the folks can (and do) lay the, "I know, I've been there…" shtick on you. Parents have not only been where you are, they've been where you're going! So they can (and do) add, "…wait'll you grow up" to the other phrase. This one-upmanship never goes over big with a teenager because there's no way to counter. Which, of course, makes you want to try.

The reason for your contrariness is a misguided effort to establish your self-worth. And there's no doubt about it – it's difficult to assert your individuality, your independence when you are 1) dependent on parents for food, shelter, and clothes, and 2) subject to a society that gives you no voice in your own affairs. That, of course, is what stimulates various forms of teenage rebellion. And that's why teenagers only feel at home with their own kind (someone no more than a year younger or older – a very narrow range of friends), and slavishly follow anyone who sympathizes with their predicament: as Dylan and the Beatles did in the 1960s, and as Springsteen, U2, and Sting do now.

There are other influences affecting the relationship between parents and teenagers that you can't do anything about except to understand them; and in understanding, to be tolerant of them (knowing you'll find yourself in the same boat in due time). A schism develops between parents and offspring after puberty. Whether or not your parents know it, or want to be reminded of it, they frequently have difficulty accepting your new-found sexuality. Dealing with the subject on a purely physical plane, the problem is that your sexual development outstrips your emotional and intellectual development. That's what's so awkward about teen years; you've got the body of an adult, the same physical needs and desires, but you lack (to varying degrees) the ability to handle it.

Imagine the effect this has on your poor parents. One minute you were a totally dependent trusting, loving little person and now you're suddenly looking and, in some respects, acting like them! It's not just a sense of loss the parent experiences – it's confusion. Until just now, you looked like a child and they looked like adults. Now the differences have vanished. It's the natural order of things to grow. But to most parents, it is disquieting – whether or not they recognize it. Parents often have a hard time handling this new reality. So their usual response is to repress and deny what Nature has provided you. Most teenage maladies flow therefrom: alienation, mistrust, shame, frustration, resentment, stammering, furtiveness, and mumbling.

That's just the way it is. Everyone goes through it. Most get through it without getting themselves so tied up in knots that it takes the next twenty years to get straightened out. If it wasn't such a tricky business, there'd be no need for books like this.

Notes to Myself

Notes to Myself

9

Problems

You've got 'em. He's got 'em. She's got 'em. They've got 'em.
Everybody's got 'em. Always have. Always will.

Life is problems. Or, more properly, life is about handling problems. It's like we each have a certain capacity for problems. Some of us have a one-quart capacity. Some have a ten-gallon capacity. Whatever it is, it's always full...of problems. When your problem level is lowered briefly because you got rid of a problem, some other problem rushes in to fill the empty space. So don't go around thinking you have these certain problems and when they're out of the way, it'll be clear sailing. The worst mistake of all is to think that after you are through with growing-up problems, and through with getting-ahead problems, that it's downhill thereafter. The truth is you die with a full load; you die in the middle of one problem or another.

This isn't being cynical or pessimistic. Problems don't mean you can't enjoy life. Problems don't exclude fun, sex, sunshine, dignity, influence, spirituality. Problems aren't even inherently 'bad.' They are 'bad' only if we handle them badly, or allow them to do bad things to us.

So it's kind of dumb to resent problems. It's even dumber to think nobody has problems like *your* problems. Of course, it's only human to want to trade yours for somebody else's. (We always want what isn't!) Poor people would gladly trade the problems of poverty for the problems of wealth. Kids would love to have a grown-up's problems, and vice versa. That leads to another rule. A small problem is a big problem when it's the only problem you have. Thus it's possible to feel as strongly about your acne as your dad feels about his bankruptcy. Acne is what's happening to you. Going broke is his thing.

Some experts on the human condition feel that problems are always with us because they are necessary for growth. Just like handling weights makes muscles grow, handling problems makes your humanity grow. Of course you can grow better (more able to cope), and you can grow worse (less able). So learning how to handle the problems of living is rather a good thing to know. And we won't hesitate to give you a few terrific pointers.

However, before that, let's acknowledge another point of view about why everyone always has problems: the notion is that problems are constant because of the way people play the game of living. The rules of the game state that *what isn't is more important (or desirable) than what is*.

That's probably because what we are and what we have seems so little, so limiting – whereas what we are not and have not is so limitless; an endless shopping list. Being dissatisfied with what is and valuing what isn't may have at its root a lack of self-esteem. The psychology being, "If *I* have it, it must not be worth much" or, "If *I* can do it, it must not be anything special." It's true that a trapese artist is not amazed at his derring-do, anymore than a surgeon is thunderstruck at what his fingers can do. We do tend to depreciate or take for granted what we do or have while being terribly impressed or covetous with our neighbor's possessions and abilities. Familiarity does seem to breed contempt.

You should also be aware that desiring what isn't requires a knowledge of what could be. Discontent is caused by an awareness of alternatives. It's when you see displays of other people's wealth that your poverty becomes a 'problem.' Which explains why dissatisfaction is so rife in this electronic age: TV has allowed millions to see what they lack. In 1932 an Alabama sharecropper had little or no contact with the world beyond his peanut patch. He didn't know what he was missing. But now he does. Now his kids do, too. This isn't all bad, of course. Matter of fact, being made aware of other possibilities is the very basis of improving the quality of one's life. You've got to know you're in jail, that there is an 'outside,' before you can value and obtain your freedom.

Down through the ages, each new generation has been confronted with problems unique to that particular time. Until recent times, most of the problems faced by young people involved staying alive long enough to become old people. A few hundred years ago, disease and hunger kept the average lifespan below forty years. The old days were not only nasty, brutish, and short, they were also boring for 99% of the populace. If your father was a herder of sheep, herding sheep was what you did forevermore (unless you were conscripted into some army and went marching off to be slaughtered). If your father was a tradesman or a craftsman, a beggarman or a thief, you were destined to be one or the other. There was no escape. Forget about seeking your fortune, fulfilling your destiny. Birthright determined all. Nothing else was possible, nothing else was expected. So while a guttersnipe may not have enjoyed life in the gutter, there was no anxiety, no stress and frustration – that's a modern day problem, caused by freedom of choice.

Your generation is confronted with its own set of unique problems (what psychologists prefer to call 'challenges'), many of them life and death matters. Life, today, bears little resemblance to life 500 or 1,000 years ago. But death is death, then and now. Then, as now, death was the ultimate problem. Only now, the thing that may kill one may kill everyone: AIDS, a nuclear hola-cust, or melting polar ice caps. Whereas people died one at a time in the olde days; these daze whole cities die in a flash (and in our arsenals we have a flash capable of wiping out all life on the planet...several times!). While each individual can die only once, who wants to die *en masse?* There would be no one left to morn our passing!

In bygone days, a teenager's problems were the same as an adult's because in those days teenagers were middle-aged: they worked like adults, went to war like adults, married and raised children like adults. So a poll of medieval teenage problems would have listed 'food,' 'warmth,' 'shelter,' or 'sickness.'

Every problem is an individual problem. Even if it's a com-mon problem, like drugs, it doesn't feel common to the sufferer. So let's avoid creating a shopping list of 'common problems' and concentrate, instead, on solutions.

Notes to Myself

Notes to Myself

10

Solutions

Rx for whatever's bugging you.

The title of this chapter may be a bit misleading. Reading this won't rid your face of zits, nor will it improve your grades or make the dope pushers disappear from your neighborhood. (Each of those problems has a solution, but you won't find it here, else we'd have to add a few thousand more pages!). This chapter is more about techniques for handling your problems – whatever they might be.

How do you remain erect while carrying a full load of problems on your back? Number one, don't expect to unload them.

The person who thinks tomorrow is going to be problem-free is going to be let down, disappointed. Burdens become unbearable when you expect to get them off your backs. (Just like 'waiting' becomes unbearable when you expect the wait to be over every next moment.) Once you face the fact that if it isn't one thing it's another, you can develop a posture that will help you bear the constant burden. If you're always thinking you're going to be unburdened tomorrow you have no incentive to learn how to carry a load of problems through life without it distorting you.

There are techniques for carrying problems effortlessly. People who have a way of smiling in the face of adversity know something. What they know, consciously or intuitively, is that they are above their problems. This isn't to deny the problem or pretend it isn't serious. A person can be serene even in the face of great pain or certain death. Because he knows this isn't happening to his self. Not the self that counts. Not the self who is trying to rise above the problems. He has detached his conscious self from his physical, ego-self.

This has nothing to do with trances or other mumbo jumbo. It has to do with altering your consciousness simply by realizing it is separate from what is happening to the body and ego. When you realize that you can literally rise above whatever is bothering you, you can detach yourself from it so that you can observe or witness it happening to the physical you. As long as you are observing, you are not totally involved. The idea isn't to deny what is happening or to treat it lightly. Lots of happenings are pretty painful. But when you know it's possible to lose a leg without losing any part of the ongoing conscious you, then you know your conscious self is different from your physical self. People who know that don't become hopelessly entangled with what's happening to their ego and body.

When you are totally caught up in what's happening, so that all of you is involved, you lose control of the situation. That's what anger does: it makes you lose control of you. You become a leaf in the wind.

To bear witness to a problem, in order to rise above it, is as simple as discussing it with yourself or God – it amounts to the same thing. Do not discuss it emotionally with wringing hands. Discuss it like a third party would discuss your problem. That's all witnessing is. Again, it may not banish your problems, but it makes them bearable, even light; not because of what you said to yourself in the discussion, but because you talked it over with yourself. That proves there's a part of you that remains enough apart from the action to be able to discuss it! Realizing that is all you need 'do.'

To reduce all this theory to practice, let's say you've been selected to address your school's student body. You agreed to do it several weeks ago when it didn't seem like much of a threat. But now, there you are listening to the principal introduce you to all those kids who've come just to watch you suffer. You start to panic…your mind races ahead picturing all the ways you're going to embarrass yourself. You're convinced your legs won't support you. Your stomach feels like it's going to lose your lunch. Now you're nervous about being nervous. That's called losing control, letting fears take over. At this point, it does no good to know that your ego-self is running the show, that you're afraid of not being admired. You've only got about three minutes to get yourself under control. To do that you've got to stop your mind from picturing all the bad things that could happen. You do that simply by experiencing the fact that you are being fearful. You say to yourself, "Wow, I'm being afraid. Look at my sweaty palms." You notice how your stomach feels. As you experience or witness what's happening to you, it will stop happening in the process. That's because you've detached your consciousness from what's happening to your physical package. Your mind is full of noticing how fear is affecting you, which leaves no room for being fearful. In the middle of noticing or experiencing what's happening, you'll find yourself on your feet talking and the rest will take care of itself. It really works – just that easily.

You can experience away anything that's bothering your mind or body. 'Anything' is pretty broad: some things (like illness) are more resistant than other things (like romantic problems).

Another example: let's say you're late for a very important date. You're on a two-lane country road stuck behind a farmer with a truck full of chickens, going twenty miles an hour. There is no place to pass. Your stomach is churning. Your head starts to throb. How you hate that guy in his pickup truck. You have three choices. Try to pass and maybe kill yourself and/or others – which is dumb. Stay in line and get madder and madder. Or you can decide to experience what is happening to you, witness yourself getting mad. Describe to yourself how it's affecting your stomach, how it's making your pits sweat. Inspect your headache: is it a pointed, sharp pain or a dull, blunt pain? Is it purplish or is it flaming red? You can't be angry while experiencing your anger. When you concentrate on what's happening to you now (madness), you can't focus on what's going to happen a few minutes from now (late-ness). You've detached yourself from the problem.

When you decide to be conscious of your fears, angers, pains, you've got them licked. Mind over matter. Just tell your self what's happening to your self and in the process that happening will either go away or fail to upset you.

Another way to one-up the problems of living has more to do with an attitude than a technique. If you'll stop and think, there are darn few moments when NOW isn't okay. You can be in the middle of a huge problem: you've just been thrown off the team because of failing grades, or you are awaiting trial for shop-lifting, or your dad's on the way home and when he sees what you did to the car, you're going to be grounded for months – but the fact is, right *NOW* is okay. *NOW* is always okay. Like right *NOW* as you read this page. Isn't it okay right *NOW*? You aren't in pain right *NOW*, are you? You aren't starving to death right *NOW*. You aren't *NOW* being insulted or made fun of. Maybe it wasn't okay yesterday, maybe you won't be okay in an hour from *NOW*. But right *NOW*, there's nothing wrong.

You could be flat broke with a heavy date coming up in six hours. If that makes you feel non-okay, it's because you are antici-pating a moment when you won't feel okay. But that's not *NOW*. That will be when you are standing in front of some cash register with empty pockets. And even when that horrible moment ar-rives and it turns out to be exactly the way you feared it would be – that *NOW* will be so filled with activity, you won't be asking yourself if it's good or bad. You'll be busy handling the situation.

People don't stop in the middle of a battle after receiving a bullet in the shoulder and say, "Hey, this *NOW* is not good." Those few *NOW*s that are non-okay take care of themselves – they are action '*NOW*s.' The *NOW*s that are noticeable are the private, passive, contemplative *NOW*s. And yet those are the moments people use to make themselves miserable. The controllable *NOW*s are the ones that get out of control. The reason we turn them from being okay to being miserable is that we use those *NOW*s to remember past non-okay *NOW*s and/or we anticipate upcoming unpleasantnesses. We only fear what isn't...yet. Like you fear there's a burglar downstairs. If and when you come face to face with a burglar, you'd be too busy reacting to have time for fear. Fright or fear arrives before and after the fact. So if you don't use your *NOW*s to fear future *NOW*s, all your *NOW*s will be okay. Okay?

Notes to Myself

11

S-E-X

Sex is like Chinese cooking...

In case you haven't noticed, S-E-X is an emotionally charged subject. Most authorities agree (and anyone who has ever felt sexy and done something about it is an authority!) that sex is, to begin with, devoid of love; in other words, a physical or biological urge.† Because sex is instinctive, it's fair to consider it natural.

But you may well wonder how come something so basic and natural has become so entangled in convention, morals, religion, custom, laws, prejudice...how come wars are fought over it, marriages break up on account of it, kids run away from home and people are put in prison because of it? How could something this spontaneous and necessary become so all-fired complicated? An excellent question.

---

†An urge being an involuntary desire that involves none of the higher emotions that separate *Homo sapiens* from barnyard animals.

The answer is that humankind is the only species that strives to control the body; to transcend the physical.

We are always involved in a great tug-of-war with physical needs and desires pulling us to one side, and metaphysical forces pulling in the opposite direction. Lower animal forms have no such problem: with them it's all eat, drink, sniff, snooze, fight, and mate.

So far in man's evolution, the physical forces have won most of the tugging contests. This is understandable. Consider that until just fifty to one hundred years ago, life was a purely a physical battle for the great mass of people. Getting enough to eat and drink consumed most of people's time. Only just recently have the masses had time apart from merely surviving (so-called 'leisure time') to contemplate, witness and develop the non-physical side of their nature.

It is man's greater purpose to rise above his physical bounds, to cut the ropes and jettison the weights that keep us tied down to the physical level; a reality men share with dogs. (What's so disquieting about barnyard sex is the similarity with our own sexual behavior – is that all we are?!) When any physical desire dominates us, whether it's food or sex, we are kept back, held down.

Do not get the idea that sex is wrong or bad or something to be denied. However, sex that treats the other person like a tree trunk is purely selfish. But the funny thing about self-gratification is – it never gratifies. Like a Chinese dinner, you keep wondering if you've missed the main course. When we seek to gratify our physical urges using another person – that is known as 'lust.' The reason lust is considered unworthy is because it is selfishly motivated. When lust drives us, we are least discriminating, least compassionate, least patient, least gentle, least human, and. . . least satisfied! Men (and women, too) lie, cheat, grovel, clown, and otherwise reduce themselves to subhuman status to gratify that physical hankering. And when it's all over, we feel somehow 'wrong' about it: embarrassed, distressed, and compromised. We feel this way not because society says it's wrong or bad or any of that. There's no such thing as a bad orgasm, physically speaking. What's incomplete about a selfish orgasm is that it only satisfies our physical half. The fact that it leaves us feeling incomplete is that our other side, our conscious side, wasn't invited to the party. It's still hungry for something more.

The kind of sex that satisfies both sides of our nature is more properly termed 'making love.' You 'make love' with someone you care about, someone you can relate to. When the parties feel an ongoing affection for each other, the sexual encounter is enhanced by the knowledge that one's partner not only enjoys your body but your 'you'! That's what's behind the female's oft-spoken complaint that, "…men only want me for my body." What she's trying to tell you, fellas, is that there is more to her than legs, breasts, lips, butts, and arms. When that's all a boy is after – an orgasm ends it. One moment he's acting like a bull, and the next he's a shrinking violet. If the only thing he and his partner had in common was the urge to merge – what's there to say and do afterwards? To avoid that awkwardness, boys usually find some excuse to leave the scene, which is why some men find paying for sex so convenient. The person who pays isn't expected to hang around and pretend to care for what's inside the body next to him.

What this all adds up to is, 'making love' is better than 'having sex,' because when there is an ongoing affection between the participants (an affection for the way the other person acts, thinks, and feels, as well as looks), the physicalness is more intense and the aftermath is beautiful. Our barnyard friends aren't capable of loving – as witness the fact that there is no aftermath when they mate. No snuggling and cooing. The rooster struts away, crowing, selfish to the end.

More than likely you've only experienced 'selfish' sex. So you probably don't know what 'it' feels like when there's a deep-seated affection for the personality operating the other body. The reason you haven't experienced that side of sex is because that kind of affection usually hasn't developed between 16-year-olds. You're too new at being grown-up. You're too full of discovering your own new fully-developed body (and those of your friends).

To be blunt about it, you haven't had enough time in the world of grown-up bodies. Your consciousness has some catching up to do. This is really what's behind the age-old prohibition against young people 'doing it.'

Most of the people who concern themselves with enforcing those prohibitions are not consciously motivated by the above awareness. There is, nevertheless, an unconscious wisdom at work that has led adults of all generations to advise against or disapprove of 'adolescent sex'; knowing that it only idealizes the physical experience, which immobilizes man's and woman's better side.

It is impossible to talk about s-e-x without mentioning the problem of AIDS. *Problem?!* It's a full-fledged disaster. A global catastrophe…the Black Plague of our times.

Christianity's punitive wing calls it, "the wages of sin," "divine retribution." How mean. How un-Christian. Maybe they'll be less judgemental now that the disease has crossed the tracks from the gay side of town and infected straight neighborhoods. Until some scientific Lone Ranger rides to our rescue and blasts the bug with a silver bullet, it's going to kill lots and lots of innocent people; most of them young. And its social side effects – causing people to withdraw from one another, to become more distrustful, defensive, suspicious, self-pleasing – may leave an even worse footprint on the human psyche. One thing's for sure: AIDS' looming shadow places a premium on fidelity, self-control, the precaution of protection…and knowing thy partner.

Notes to Myself

Notes to Myself

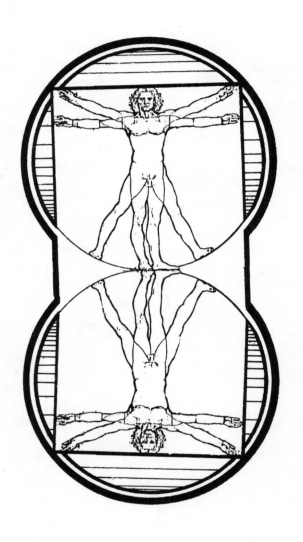

12

Highs and Lows

What are you, a yo-yo?

You probably have another sixty to seventy years to live
with that body of yours. So any habits you pick up at this age are
going to hang around for a long, long time. That's one reason it's
sad to see teenagers take up smoking, drinking and all the rest.

You are into a discovery period...a time of life when you are
emerging from the cocoon of childhood into an adult form. It's a
shame to have you take off on your maiden flight with a broken
wing. At this moment your systems are finely tuned: your sense of
smell, sight, hearing, your ability to run, jump and be joyful will
never again be what they are now. Your present physical high is
heightened by a natural psychic receptiveness that makes the
teenage years a natural high.

Perhaps it is this unbounded exuberance, this innocent
enthusiasm, this eagerness to sample and experiment that leads so

many young people to assume they can handle anything and
everything. Whatever the reason, the fact is *there is never a time
when you have so much to lose and so little to gain by playing around
with substances that only bring you down from where you are now.*

Sure, you've got all these frustrations, complaints, problems. If you've been reading along, you know you're no different
in that regard. The only thing that's different about teenage
problems is that you're better equipped to handle them – you've
got the physical stamina, the optimism, and confidence of youth
going for you. All the more reason not to introduce unnecessary
outside forces into the mix.

That's what inspires this manual – the hope that we might
say something that will steer you away from pitfalls adults have
placed in your path. (Kids didn't invent booze, cigarettes, coke,
crack, LSD and the like.) Teenagers turn to that stuff with the
misguided belief it will either help overcome what's bugging
them or make what's good even better.

You can always take up smoking, drinking, and drugging.
You can start next year or in five or thirty years from now. It's always your choice. Try holding out for a while. (Even if you think
you're missing something good. If it's good now, it'll be good
later.) Once you do anything for the first time, it will never be
new again. As life moves on, you will be hard pressed for new

experiences. So save a few for later. (You may discover they aren't needed.)

Okay, time to lay a few bummers on you. As a convenience to the writer, you'll find pills lumped with pot, and booze with tobacco, and horse with coke, although they each are separate cases involving different risks and legal sanctions. Anyway, we're not here to discuss the chemistry of grass or the sanity of laws governing its use. One chapter is hardly up to all that. So, if you'll forgive us doing an occasional injustice to one or the other substance, we'd like to proceed, first from the legal angle.

It is lamentable that society has decided to deal with drug abuse as a criminal matter rather than a psychological or medical problem. Actually, that's why drunkenness, dope addiction, lewd conduct and other victimless crimes have been made crimes. Society finds it much more convenient and comfortable dealing with criminals than it does handling alcoholics, drug users, and flashers. But whether or not the statutes governing the uses of 'harmful' substances are enlightened or not, the penalties are real. And one of the penalties there's no avoiding: the law has caused the marketing of these substances to go underground. And there you are obliged to deal with some pretty un-nice characters.

One of the un-nice services performed by dealers is to turn you on to pills when they are out of grass, or when a couple of big

busts drives the price beyond your pocketbook. There's no independent grass market – it's one big supermarket. You know about
supermarkets – that's where people buy on impulse. The only connection between grass and LSD, coke and heroin is the marketing
connection.

Addiction is another reality. Addiction is hellish. You have
heard all the horror stories, so we'll save you that. All we want to
say about addiction is, "*Who needs it?*" There's nothing more pre-
cious than 1) freedom: being unattached, free from strings, and 2)
good health. When you become attached to anything – drugs, tobacco, booze, money, self-pity, sex – you have limited your freedom, your choice. Of course, everyone says, "Not *me*," just like every US Marine who stormed the beaches of Iwo Jima said, "They
won't kill *me*...Tom, Dick or Harry, maybe, but not *me*." That's the
only way the Marines could sell anyone on leaving that landing
craft – the same way it's the only way you could be sold on am-
phetamines or heroin.

The fact is, once you start, you've got an excellent chance of
becoming somebody's yo-yo. As we said early on, what's sad is you
didn't really *need* it. You weren't dying for a drink, hungering for a
cigarette, desperate for a pep pill. You never need the first one!
Why go to all that trouble, expense and worry to learn how to
need something? Especially when *the less you need the freer you are*.
Just as Bob Dylan says, "the less you got, the less you got to lose."

Then there's the matter of your physical well-being, your health. Good health is taken for granted, especially by teenagers who think that's all there is, and it's forever. Maybe you don't know what bad health is like. Sooner or later you will, but make it later if you can because nothing is good when you feel bad. Money, sex, food...all the bodily pleasures go sour. And it's all the more difficult to handle life's problems when you're feeling crappy. When your body is screaming, you can't hear the birds singing.

There's another kind of addiction besides physical. Grass is a good example of the more subtle kind of hook. When you become psychologically dependent on anything outside of yourself to make you feel better or more capable, you in effect have given up control of yourself. Every joint you light is an admission (that registers in your psyche, admitted or not) that your 'you' is inadequate. Each event registers as a personal defeat. Just a tiny little chip in your self-confidence, perhaps, but considering the number of years you've got to go – don't be too casual. That's how they cut down giant redwoods, a chip at a time.

Self-confidence is necessary for self-esteem. When you lack that, you're asking for trouble. (People who have no self-esteem cause most of the trouble – for themselves and others.) And it's pretty hard to get yourself out of trouble when you don't esteem yourself. A double whammy. The guy who gets drunk to get up the nerve to 'make-out' has just tied drink to sex. It quickly grows into a *goeswith* situation. But the man who says, "It's going to be me who does it, not booze" is going to increase his confidence in himself. Even if he's unsuccessful, he doesn't lose what he would have, had he 'made it' on booze.

And what makes you think sights, sounds, and feelings are made better by drugs, much less liquor? What you see, hear, and feel is what *you* see, hear, and feel. If a drug can sharpen your senses, you can sharpen your senses by conscious effort. All the hallucinogenics do is direct or focus your consciousness. There's nothing they can do that you can't do on your own – it's just a matter of deciding to – deciding to be more conscious of the music; to hear all its colorations and nuances. Those drugs just make you more conscious *unconsciously.* Not much self-satisfaction in that. You didn't do it. The drug did. Your 'you' is diminished.

Because these 'lectures' always come from adults, and because adults are well-known killjoys – teenagers get the feeling; that the adult world is against everything that feels good, that anything good is bad. Unfortunately, too many grownups do tend to resent the pleasure-orientation of youth. It's kind of a sour grapes attitude.

But don't write off *all* advice that comes from the other side of 30. Jumping off a cliff and soaring like a bird might appear to be a desirable experience to someone who doesn't know about wings and gravity. Adults have experienced falling; so when we see someone heading for a fall, it's difficult not to issue a warning.

Notes to Myself

13

Kamikaze Kids

Teenagers are becoming an endangered species.

The teen years are a high-risk age: always have been, always will be. But in recent years the risks are getting out of hand. In just this past decade, the per capita death rate, accidental and otherwise, among US teenagers has increased by more than 500%.

Learning to fly involves crash landings, true. But your generation of high-flyers are crashing with such regularity that the cause must be something more than bad luck, poor training or faulty equipment. Many of the crack-ups seem intended! At least they are not unexpected.

Why this flirtation with death? Why are so many teenagers acting like there's no tomorrow – drinking, driving, drugging yourselves into oblivion? And why now?

Teenage suicide is up 300% in the last five years! And that
doesn't account for the kids who've used an automobile, drugs,
etc., to kill themselves.

Violence accounts for more than 75% of all adolescent
deaths. And almost all that 'violence' is related to drinking and
substance abuse: vehicle accidents, over-dosing, physical attacks,
and suicides. That's doubly shocking, because – by definition –
those deaths were avoidable, unnecessary! If former friends of
yours contributed to these statistics – that only makes the loss
more tragic. They weren't the victims of a some unavoidable virus,
a battlefield casualty, struck down by a bolt out of the blue. Most
likely, your friends didn't have to die! Whatever happened was
invited, knowingly or not. Driving like a madman tanked up on
beer or whatever, scoring drugs in a dark part of town – these go
beyond risky. It's akin to suicide; slower than a bullet, but it hurts
more. Of course, you know that. But did they? If they didn't, the
solution would be so easy: force every teenager in the country to
read what you're reading. Simple as that! Trouble is – it isn't as
simple as that, is it? There isn't anyone who buys or sells dope that
doesn't know they're doing something bad/wrong (which goes to
make it good/right in some people's minds). Have you ever met a
drunk driver who, when sober, recommended driving drunk? No,
most of the victims knew better. But that didn't stop them.

Preventative measures usually fail because they focus on symptoms rather than causes. "Just say 'No'" may be a good slogan, but it doesn't address the reasons kids say "Yes."† Drugs, liquor, promiscuous sex aren't the problem – any more than teenagers are the problem. (You're the victim!)

One answer to all the 'whys' being asked may be this: more teenagers are being 'burned' (compared to past generations), because today's teenagers have more matches to play with; all different kinds, many of them new kinds that burn faster, hotter, longer – all designed by your elders! It's the matches that are different. Twenty-five years ago dope wasn't so accessible and acceptable, nor was it so powerful. Fifty years ago automobiles weren't teenage playthings. One hundred years ago this was an agrarian

---

† Wouldn't you agree that most teenagers say "Yes" to fit-in; to avoid being left out? But in truth, "Yes" is a sign of weakness, an admission you lack the self-confidence to act on your own, to be your own boss, to do what you want to do rather than what others want you to do. Teenagers are always moaning about having their lives run by adults, yet when decisions are left to you, you let the crowd decide! Teenagers haven't had much practice saying, "No." So before you find yourself in a "Yes" or "No" situation, prepare yourself – practice saying "No" gracefully, without making a big deal of it. It doesn't have to be a loud "No" that will cause all the "Yes" people to get down on you. At a time like that, you aren't trying to make them 'wrong.' You're just speaking for yourself. If a simple "No" seems too short, try "No, thanks. I don't drink." Or, if that sounds too negative, try, "I'll pass." Or just say you're having a good time already. (No one can get mad at that!) The point is, have a "No" answer ready. Because people often say "Yes" because they didn't know how to say "No."

society. While the problems discussed here are unique to an urban-suburban society.

So don't get the feeling that yours is a failed generation. (If anyone's a failure, it's the generation in front you!) You didn't create the economic problems that compromise the quality of your future life. You didn't invent booze, crack, grass, tobacco, the internal combustion engine, aerosol sprays, or sex. (You just discovered them!)

Every generation has its own set of worries. But unlike generations past, the problems you'll be saddled with are capable of wiping out the future; e.g., THE BOMB hangs over your heads, AIDS lurks under your beds, and melting ice caps threaten to turn your hometown into Venice.

These are monumental problems, no doubt about it. But being manmade, they can be solved by man. You aren't going to solve the world's problems at sweet 16. Right now, all you need to do is stay healthy, physically and mentally. The reason you should do that is because *there will be a tomorrow*. No matter how painful your present, you have a lot to live for...more than you can possibly imagine. And that goes for kids who have it a lot worse than you: kids forced to live like animals in an urban jungle, to say nothing of teenagers trapped in foreign hellholes like Ethiopia and the Middle East. Many of them won't be around when tomorrow comes. At least you have a choice.

You may choose to stumble through your formative years stoned, like a zombie. You can choose to whine and complain about the mess the adult world has left for you to clean up. You can lay down and wallow in it, or roll up your sleeves and clean it up. It's your choice: to be part of the problem...or the solution.

One thing's for sure, tomorrow will not resemble today. It will not include today's problems and pains. So grit your teeth and hang on for dear life – today's problems will be tomorrow's memories. Guaranteed. Soon you'll find yourself someplace totally new, with new friends, new everything. Come 21 it's a whole new ballgame, a fresh start, a new race. Those who win will be those who enjoy running. Those who use all their energy complaining usually fall by the wayside, too exhausted to keep up.

Fear of Flying

"Stop the world, I want to get off!"

The flight crew that's piloted Spaceship Earth through the 1950s, 60s, 70s and 80s will be replaced in the 1990s with a brand new crew – you. That old crew will be turning over a planet that's been over-revved, under-maintained, and planted with the seeds of its own destruction. So the new flight crew better be made of 'the right stuff' to get everything back in good working order.

Trouble is, many of you who should be attending flight school right now are AWOL; so it's going to be a small graduating class that possesses the technical skills and mental toughness. What's more, many of you who are fit for duty, don't want the duty, preferring to go along for a free ride in first class. Then, as soon as the ride gets a little bumpy, you start strapping on parachutes and pushing the panic button! Before you jump, there are a few things to consider, like where are you going to land once you've left Earth.

Notes to Myself

14

Rx for those "Nothing-to-Live-for Teenage Blues"

Hope for the hopeless, help for the helpless.

He was 16, good lookin', bright, and well-liked. Jason lived in a big house in a small town full of sunshine and affluence. His dad was a honcho, his mom a talented, loving lady. Jason's older brother and sister each had a wall full of athletic and scholarship honors. Everything they touched turned to success. Just as much was expected of Jason, maybe more. Oh, his parents didn't push it, they didn't require it. It was just – well, expected, assumed. Most of the pressure was of his own making. Jason expected a lot from himself, and no doubt he expected that his parents, brother and sister, relatives and friends were also expecting great things from the last in line. After all, he had all the advantages, all the right equipment and accessories – how could he fail? But he did. Nothing horrible: he didn't flunk any courses, get anyone pregnant, or run amok in a convent – nothing like that. He just wasn't doing great. He wasn't nearly as successful as his brother and sister were at his age. That bothered Jason, bothered him a lot. A lot more than anyone knew. He covered up his concern with smiles and jokes, beers and parties, a joint after school (which led to tokes between classes, which led him to miss classes, then whole days!).

Then his dealer 'friend' laid some coke on him. Oh, wow, how good he felt. It covered up his worries like booze, only faster – made everything just fine…until he ran out.

Replenishing his supply proved too expensive for a 16-year old's allowance. So Jason sold his expensive mountain bike. That bought him enough cocaine to last for…ever.

When that ran out, Jason was frantic – hyper – which probably contributed to the accident. It was his dad's car. *Trés* expensive, *mucho dinero*. Father was outta town, fortunately (or unfortunately). His mother 'lent' him the money to have it fixed. Instead, Jason spent the money on a different kind of fix.

The last time his friends saw Jason was after school (they hadn't seen him during school for days). They remember he was in "an awful state," strung out from a three-day cocaine bout. But still smiling, still joking – everything was still okay; all he needed was sleep, he said.

Jason went home, lay down with a shotgun and slept forever.

All that happened a few years ago. Had Jason slept alone, woke up and faced his parents' shock and disappointment, the brotherly lectures – he would have been able to turn his life around. He would have discovered he had what it takes after all. He would be in his middle-20s now. Out of college, into a career, married maybe, no longer feeling inferior to his older brother and sister, returning to the big house for reunions, and hanging out with old high school friends remembering the good ol' days.

Maybe next time, Jason...

For those of you reading this – leave yourself a 'next time,' however painful the present time may be. When it gets real bad...when life is a misery that keeps getting worse, and all you can think of is escape – hang in there, hang on for dear life. One Jason is one too many.

Knowing how these tragedies happen might help to stop them from happening.

No pain is the same. Everyone hurts differently, for different reasons. When there's physical pain combined with mental anguish – like Jason's – you are particularly vulnerable to panic. Your mind runs out of control; you don't want to control it, preferring to feed the fires that are burning your insides. At that point, people can't help themselves – they're their own worst enemies. Hopefully, someone will be there to lead you out of harm's way. If not, the front of the phone book is full of help. For God's sake – open it. Talk before you act.

Success comes easy for the successful. Contrariwise, once you start a downward spiral, it's hard to pull out – and so easy to just let yourself go

down

down

down until you're so far down in the dumps no one can reach you. So you've got to catch yourself before you reach the bottom.

People who get down on themselves spend too much time alone with themselves. That creates a vacuum in which negative thoughts flourish. It's even worse to hang out with a bunch of downers, kids with the same complaints. They'll only reinforce your depressed, negative view. If you can't involve yourself with a happy, confident, active crowd – strangers will do. Just get out, expose yourself to someplace new. Take a bus to wherever it goes. Surround yourself with crowds, upbeat music. Attend a sporting event. Best of all – run, run, and run some more. Don't ask why. Just do it. When your body is running, your mind isn't.

There are other tactics, all designed to occupy your mind. When it's unoccupied it'll turn on you every time. Whose mind is it, anyway? It exists to do the bidding of your super consciousness. But once your mind gains control of the consciousness – it has a mind of its own.

Let's hope you never go through this personal hell, yet a friend of yours may. But they are not likely to tell you. You'll have to sense their turmoil. It seldom shows. So many times someone seemed to be acting normally and the next thing you hear – they did this crazy thing. If only you had known...

Most suicides can be stopped. (Preventing a re-occurrence is another matter – a professional matter.) Especially teenage suicides. They're not beyond reach – they're probably teetering, going through a "Should I, or shouldn't I?" argument. Their doubt is your ally; their life preserver.

They are one step from eternity. That's no time or place to argue with them. Sympathize, even agree with 'em... whatever it takes to give life a chance. Always give life a chance. Just a day. If they feel like this today, stand the pain one more day, to make sure they still feel the same way tomorrow.

None of the above deals with their reasons.† It's emergency first-aid. Aid first; the time for remedies is later.

Remember, life is full of agonies and ecstasies, ups and downs. When you're down, it'll seem like you'll never ever be up again. And when a teenager is down, it may be for the first time. So it will be the furthest down you've ever been. And because you haven't experienced the way life turns around, you don't think it will. That's breeds hopelessness. But that isn't going to happen to you. Because you've read this book; you know *where there's life, there's hope.* Something better is always around the corner. So press on, regardless…

There are going to be so many changes in your lifetime; so many turnarounds. Insurmountable troubles will be surmounted. Unbearable pain will be borne. Someone with nothing to live for soon has everything to live for. It happens all the time. Two recent examples follow – read and reap:

---

† They are seldom dissuaded by reason. Suicide contradicts all reason, all wisdom. No other creature self-destructs. It's against nature, unnatural. It makes no sense so you can't be sensible about it. To be capable of suicide, to over-ride Nature's life preservation systems, a person must necessarily be temporarily insane (from pain, grief, despondency, hopelessness, shame, whatever). Oftentimes,

A 30-year-old South American labor leader is thrown into a dungeon and tortured. Day after day, year after year he wanted to die but couldn't. The only thing worse than today would be to-morrow. Ten years later he is living in San Francisco, healthy, wealthy, a loving family around him – his captors punished. Give it time, it will work out.

A Laotian tribesman loyal to the US cause is captured by the Viet Cong. His family is murdered. He's tortured, mutilated, starved, and spends years penned-up in a 5'x 5' bamboo cage Finally he escapes and reaches the sea, swims to a fishing boat, wakes up in friendly territory. He comes to the US, where he is now the successful owner of fifteen car washes.

Life is full of such turnarounds. Your reprieve may be in the mail. To end one's own life is to play God. You are passing judgement on future events you have no way of foretelling. Never give up.

---

suicide is a negative, vindictive act – a way of paying back those causing your pain: parents, some unrequited love, or just some faceless 'they' or 'them.' "They'll be sorry…," "I'll show them…" "They made me…" That's why all who jump off the Golden Gate Bridge choose the side facing land – where 'they' are.

Notes to Myself

Notes to Myself

15

You Are Not Alone

"You are home. You belong in the Universe."

—Alan Watts

We were tempted to leave this chapter out. The idea it expresses is so simple, so basic to all else, but so contrary to how things appear that it may very well confuse the hell out of you. We must risk that result because to stop short of what follows is like not dropping the other shoe. All would be incomplete without this 'secret' of the universe.

Because your consciousness is presently contained in a physical package, you get the idea that 'I' am not 'you' anymore than 'you' are not the tree you're standing under. Consequently, each of us feels separated or apart from others. Most everything we experience reinforces this illusion of separateness. The tree is not me, so it's okay to chop it down. She is not me, so it's okay to hurt her. 'They' are not me, so it's okay to hate 'them.'

All the un-good feelings that come our way – shyness, inferiority, resentment, jealousy, all that stuff – are fostered by this sense of being apart, alone in a vast alien universe. It's little ol' you against all else. No wonder you feel oppressed, inadequate, threatened, scared, confused. No wonder you 'drop out,' run and hide.

But the 'you' that appears to be separate and at war with every other object is the physical you.

If our consciousness wasn't contained in a package of flesh that takes up space and casts a shadow, your ego couldn't exist. It would have no home. The ego-you that you take to be all of you is a charade, a shadow. It is the part of you that is diminished when you lose a limb or some organ. The soldier who comes back from the wars in a wheel chair is only 'half a man,' but all he's lost are pieces of his physical facade. If he thinks that's all he is, he feels reduced: his ego feels reduced. His consciousness hasn't been reduced. That is still whole. That is indivisible, indestructible, which is to say, immortal.

Actually, everything except ego is immortal...even physical things. But the immortality of physical things is based on transformations. Bodies die and the material is recycled. Bodies are matter and matter is energy. Energy just keeps transforming itself. A leaf drops to the ground, becomes humus providing energy for new growth. All material forms of energy keep transforming. Only pure consciousness (a much higher form of energy) remains constant.

Whether or not you sense the all-important difference be-tween you as a body/ego and you as conscious awareness, make a leap of faith and accept the concept for the sake of discussion. Now we can take the next step.

Because you are not what you think you are – a separate body/ego apart from all the other separate bodies/egos – you are in fact part of the whole: *all is one and one is all.* You are everything. Everything is interdependent; not just in an ecological sense. As a great Hassidic rabbi put it, "If I am I because you are you, and if you are you because I am I, then I am not I and you are not you." Instead we are both something in common. It's as if our bodies were light bulbs. When we are plugged into electrical energy we light up. We appear to glow independently of one another (albeit some brighter, some dimmer, and some are red, yellow, white, etc.).

What's real and wondrous about a lightbulb is not the bulb but the energy the bulb transforms into light. Bulbs burn out but that energy flows on, to be tapped by other bulbs. The cosmic consciousness is that energy flow. It's always there. It's all there is. That's it. So what we have are a lot of separate bodies (separate bulbs) plugged into the one energy source. Because we don't *see* the connection – there is no see-able cord – we get the notion we are self-contained light sources with a certain life expectancy.

We don't know what got us to glowing or why, and we exist in constant fear our light will go out. What we must realize is the bulb, our body, while a wondrous device, is merely the medium, a receptacle, one means of manifesting or expressing consciousness. Because the medium has enough mass to be 'material' it suffers inevitable wear and tear, deteriorates and finally ceases to function, dies, then proceeds to transform itself into crumbled glass and oxidizing wires *en route* to becoming 'dust.'

Seeing this, other bulbs (who think all they are, are bulbs!) are wont to believe that's the end: the light went out, it's all over. While the physical manifestation isn't in fact 'over,' but is merely transforming itself into other forms of matter, the conscious element, the light source, is unaffected, undiminished by the bulb's fate. It's just that we can't *see* consciousness. We can't see it before it actualized the bulb and we can't see where it went after it no longer had the bulb to light. Because the consciousness cannot 'see' itself, anymore than you can see the back of your eyes, it's easy to be tricked into the illusion of separateness.

That's why people who wish to be released from their ego-selves retreat from the seeable world so they might better focus inward...to become more conscious of their consciousness. (Not by concentrating but by doing nothing, thinking nothing, avoiding those common activities that short circuit a full flow of energy.) Meditation is a means of opening the circuits, so you receive a full charge of current.

What does this all mean to a 16-year-old immersed in a world of separate objects, conflicting egos? The simple, sensational message this carries is that you are not alone; not an alien in an inhospitable universe. You are not in competition with or being opposed by other people or forces. Only in form are you apart. We are all plugged into the same flow. What animates your form (make it 'glow') is what makes rocks so hard and suns so shiny. So to dislike or do harm to other objects is to dislike and harm yourself. That's what makes racism so stupid. Instead of seeing others as separate lighted bulbs (of all hues), instead 'see' the common source of our light. Electricity doesn't come in colors.

But...but...*but*...you, he, her, them, us, they, we are still involved in the world of appearances, where bodies are separate and unequal and operate in opposition to one another. How to handle this world of winning and losing without denying the ultimate reality of "one is all and all is one"? The only way to handle both realities – to work both sides of the street – is to *consider living as a game*. Life is best lived in the spirit of play. To be sure, it's a game where you can suffer grievous pain, where cars run over people, where cancers prey, where cutthroats lurk. So you must pay attention to the players and rules. By realizing life's a game played by egos and objects, you have detached your consciousness from it – you can witness you 'playing' the game, simply because you are now conscious of it as a game. If you become so immersed in the game that you can't, won't, or don't witness what's happening – then you've got trouble. It's like going to a horror movie and getting so involved that you forget you are actually in the audience, a witness to the spectacle. As a result, you suffer the tortures of the damned. But isn't it nice when the lights come on. What a relief.

As long as you remain conscious of your conscious you, you can retreat from the ego-game – if only long enough to rearm yourself for the next battle. You can wade in and out like going in and out of a movie house.

Another good thing about living life as a game – it makes you appreciate the role of opposing forces. You can't have a game without winning and losing, without penalties and rewards. Opponents are an indispensable element of any game. You can't play without someone to oppose you. The game of life involves others. You know you are winning or losing, good or bad, big or small, pretty or ugly, tall or short only in relation to others. How you are doing is completely entwined with how others are doing. Knowing that, you can better practice what Jesus preached about loving your enemies. This is not to say that you should pretend they are not enemies. Love them *as* enemies...because without a 'bad guy' how could you play 'good guy'? So even in the hard-edged physical world, all things are interdependent.

One last flash about playing life as a game: this recognition keeps conflicts within bounds. Games have rules† that players must agree to. Once you recognize you are a player you can lighten up. Without that realization there could be no such thing as chivalry...the spirit that keeps warfare within limits. For if all the warring parties lacked chivalry, there would be no limits... there'd be no stopping nuclear obliteration.

"Chivalry is the noble spirit, embodied in the knight of old, who plays with his life." Chivalry is a WWI pilot with streaming silk scarf dueling in the sky, trying to shoot down the opposition but not pressing the trigger when seeing the opponent has exhausted his ammo.

People who are so attached to the game they are playing, who think they are nothing but their ego, are incapable of acting chivalrous or civilized. These are extremely dangerous folk. They

---

†There's a non-game, *i.e.*, a game with no rules governing its conduct, that people play called Anarchy, or Terrorism.

are the ones who would push the big button given the chance.
They must be played with very carefully.

So play hard, play well, but *remain aware* that you are playing. That's all you need to do. Just remain aware. That way you
can't lose even if you lose. Because you'll know you just lost a
game. That's no big deal in the cosmic scheme of things.

Notes to Myself

Notes to Myself

16

Enjoy Now

Nothing satisfies an individual incapable of enjoyment.

There is too little joy in being young. The reason there is so little joy in it is because the people who run the world, the old(er) people, are a product of a goal-oriented culture. So youth is no end unto itself; no more than a preparatory period, when one prepares for the responsibilities of adulthood. . . or so they'd have you think.

It has been said, "man is the only creature who doesn't know that the chief business of life is to enjoy it." As a species, we suffer from *pleasure anxiety*. That is, we hesitate to enjoy ourselves out of fear something bad will follow.   In other words, "it may rain on my parade so I won't march!" We have this guilty conscience about pleasure. Perhaps it's a hangover from the concept of original sin, perhaps a complex developed from centuries of stoop labor.

Whatever the reason, there's too little joy in Teensville (where the capacity is greatest!) because adults are killjoys. Pleasure-seeking, for its own sake, is definitely not the way to get on in the adult world. Here we refer to so-called pointless pleasures: the joy of running free, of singing in a crowded bus, of catching a wave, of studying a butterfly's wing.

Because adulthood seems to be the objective of youth – being young is somehow less desirable – a lower order of existence. Young people are put down when they act youthful and lauded when they act adult. The way for teenagers to win friends and influence adult people is to become goal-oriented: to begin sawing away at a violin or leafing through medical manuals; while Peter Pans are the object of concern.

Yet the truth is this: unless one is able to live fully in the present, the future is a hoax. There is no point whatever in making plans for a future which you'll never be able to enjoy. For when those plans mature, you'll still be living for some other future beyond.

You'll never be able to sit back and say, "I've arrived!" Our educational system has robbed us of this capacity because it has prepared us for the future, instead of helping us to be alive *NOW*. We have become conditioned by a processing system arranged in steps or grades supposedly leading to some ultimate success. But the steps never stop until death. (Let us hope that heaven is a footless society – where we can be still in the endless *NOW.*) The bottom line to all this is that *enjoyment is an art and a skill for which we have little talent or energy.*

Joy is not an antisocial force. Joy is not a refuge for self-indulgent, freeloading hippies. It is a beneficial state of mind. It is health-giving: joyful people are demonstrably healthier than sourpusses. And have you ever known a joy-filled person (if, indeed, you know one) who is likely to cause a war, commit a murder, have a nervous breakdown, or bear a grudge?

It's one thing to urge you to *enjoy now.* It's another thing to do it – without dropping out of the mainstream of our culture. The reality of the material world is that we are expected to work, to achieve, to progress. The trick is how to deal with the materialism that surrounds you and still be joy-filled. Keeping the discussion on that material, Reality I level, the way to do it is to find yourself a ladder that's fun to climb. Find a way of making a living or 'getting ahead' that is enjoyable in and of itself, so the process of getting to the top is worth the trip – whether or not you get there (or find another ladder awaiting you). That is the stuff of the next chapter…

Notes to Myself

Notes to Myself

17

Follow Your Bliss

Choose a job you love and you'll never have to work a day in your life.

For those of you who don't make a career of being a student, which is good work if you can get it, earning a living is what you will do (un)happily ever after.

Most men die in the saddle, and most women with a mop in hand – women's lib notwithstanding.

But between now and when working for a living becomes unavoidable, there's the question of schooling. As you may have noticed, education and achievement go hand-in-glove in our goal-oriented society. Observation would lead one to question that assumption. But let us concede that a so-called 'higher education' is a necessity for anyone pursuing a profession. And it is, we fear, fast becoming a self-perpetuating necessity for just plain 'business people,' the folks who captain our industries.

What's phoney about academic degrees is that they hardly prepare one for the realities of the marketplace. Four years (starting from scratch) in the marketing department of Procter & Gamble will make you a better marketing person than four years working with university models. The trouble is – you wouldn't get the chance to get into P & G's marketing department without a BA, probably an MBA. The reason is (though P & G would never admit it), there are so many BAs kicking around that companies always have a choice between a Mr/Ms with a masters degree or Mr/Ms without one. All else being equal, companies figure the better educated person is a safer bet than the undereducated person.

This overabundance of qualified people is growing. In the 1990's more that 40% of everyone between 20 and 40 will have a college degree, many with masters and doctorates. Considering this competition it'll be hard to launch yourself into the executive world without collegiate credentials.†

There are, however, other worlds beyond business, the sciences and humanities. There are plumbers, tool-and-dye makers, owners of hardware stores, lumberjacks and teamsters, first mates, singers, ski instructors, sanitation engineers, tillers of the soil, disc

---

†Were that not the case, we'd be inclined to advise all who do not pursue a professional career to consider using their educational funds to finance a grand tour; travel experience being a better 'finishing school' than a campus.

jockeys and horse jockeys, writers, nurserymen, steeplejacks, sign painters, clerics, warehousemen, dancers. And those people involved with 'high technology,' or what's loosely termed, 'electronics,' including the computer sciences and telecommunications. What plastics was to the 1950s, electronics is to the 1990s – a mind-boggling field of opportunity.†

When in doubt about your career, take the advice of the late Joseph Campbell, an educator *extraodinaire*, who said, "Follow your *bliss*"; or, do what you want to do. Because when you like doing something, you'll do it well. Do it even if it isn't monetarily rewarding. Because personal satisfaction is worth more than gold, and never looses its value.

Hindu philosophy says each individual has his or her *swadharma*, which means one's individual law of development. Determining what yours is means assessing a number of contributing factors. First is heredity – what you have received from your ancestors. You did not spring out of nothing, you inherited certain tendencies and impressions that exist in your subconscious. Then there is environment – the social, economic, political, religious,

---

†While this field will employ some 50 million, billions of people will employ their handiwork: computer technology. Those who don't, or can't, will form a new economic underclass. Do not join their ranks! Repeat: do not be computer illiterate. If you use school for nothing else, use it to master the microcomputer. Because if that electronic lash-up is a mystery when you graduate, you'll enter the workforce with two strikes against you.

educational, cultural, and climatic conditions under which you are reared. All these and more determine your *swadharma*. If you are compelled or persuaded to work at something contrary to your *swadharma* you will find it difficult to be successful (which includes enjoyment).

Over and above the question of *swadharma*, do not readily accept meaningless, dehumanizing, repetitive tasks, nor those that blatantly exploit the weaknesses of others. There's no satisfaction in such work, and forty or fifty years is a helluva long time to stay dissatisfied. Don't even do it for a short time because before you know it, you'll have accumulated real or imagined reasons for not being able to change course. Ruts form quickly.

This is terribly important, finding employment that isn't methodical, that doesn't rot your abilities, kill your spirit or compromise your principles. Because the only way to bear such a job is to live in the future; that is, to stop living against the hope of future advancement, financial reward and retirement.

When money becomes the sole object, the goal, you've bought yourself a one-way ticket to Nowheresville. Not because money is inherently 'evil' (it's not – it's a most convenient medium of exchange). But money makes a lousy goal. Goals should be attainable. But nobody has ever gained enough money. Money is a more-ish commodity: the more you want the more you get the more you need the more you want. Very frustrating. It's a carrot you can never get your teeth into.

It's been written, "He who wants money does not really know what he wants...his desires are limitless, and no one can tell how to deal with him." When your goal in life is something less illusive – like winning the Indianapolis 500 or becoming a Realized Being who is sustained by solar energy – you have the right kind of goal, for they are worth the trip. When you pursue such objectives you will enjoy the effort of getting there, whether or not you ever do get there. Destinations once reached often prove disappointing. If you didn't enjoy the trip, then it's been a total waste. Remember – all you can really count on is *now*. If you aren't enjoying *NOW*, you lose.

On the subject of 'goals,' we should acknowledge that there are tactical, short-range goals (such as winning at Indianapolis) and strategic or long-range goals. Strategic goals concern values or principles – the stuff that determines what manner of person you are, which determines the approach to your tactical objectives. Many if not most people are not conscious of having a strategic, lifelong goal or ruling principles. "To be happy" is the usual synthetic reply. But "being happy" is an effect, a result of being something else (like tolerant and compassionate).

Getting back to the question of avoiding uninvolving work – it should be conceded that in times of deep recession, it's not always possible to be choosey. Digging ditches is probably preferable to standing in line for food stamps (if only because this culture respects workers, while it makes nonworkers pay for their benefits by forfeiting their dignity). So, if and when you are stuck with a nothing job, apply the principle of detachment by witnessing yourself digging the ditch. Digging dirt is just what's happened to the physical you. Your body is doing the digging while you observe. Maybe you can't dig that scene, but it's the way to bear anything – including pain.

Most often though, there is work that involves your conscious you. (Drudgery lets the mind wander, and it usually wanders to feelings of self-pity and resentment.) The world is full of opportunity if you will but seek it out. If you want to write, become a fire watcher for the forest service. If you like the sun, get a lifeguard's certificate. If you like the sea, ship out. *Do what you like*. That's the best possible career advice we can give. If you don't enjoy it, you won't do it well and you will not be rewarded.

There are basically two kinds of jobs. One kind initiates, starts others in motion, makes things happen; builders, for example. The second kind reacts to the first kind, like a carpenter reacts to the builder. The builder decides to create a house, which provides the carpenter with an opportunity to ply his trade. The advertising man reacts to the needs of advertisers. Because initiators usually have more to lose, they are also in a position to make more money (for whatever that's worth), and gain the extra measure of satisfaction that comes from being the enabler, the spark plug; whereas the reactors are like gears.

Whatever you do, do it well. Give it your best. Old-fashioned advice, but sound. When any job is done poorly, you lose two ways: 1) you lose your self-respect, and 2) you lose any chance to grow and advance. Quality always seeks its proper level.

Notes to Myself

18

Go Do It

Give 100%, get 100%.

Most of society's sins are committed in a misguided effort to help people avoid failure. For instance, in the US it's pretty hard to starve to death, and even harder to fail at school. The harder the system works to ensure that everyone will eat and be educated and receive equal opportunities, the lower our standards become.

People need to take risks. It's what keeps our internal machinery running smoothly – prevents carbon buildup. When a high-revving engine is allowed to loaf mile after mile it's going to develop problems. That's what the educational system does to you; that's what the corporate management system is doing to your father!

As things now stand, it's practically impossible to fail in school. You can be caught fiddling with a live hand grenade in geometry class, and after 'suffering' a severe reprimand by the principal and promising never to do it again, you'll be back in line for a diploma. This everyone-makes-it system produces a great mass of mediocrity – a nation of half-educated people. But that's not the worst of it.

When kids don't have a proving ground that really tests their mettle, they are going to invent their own challenges, and these almost always take antisocial forms; driving like maniacs, swallowing X-rated pharmaceuticals, participating in gang wars and other forms of thrillseeking. Russian Roulette is what bored, cooped-up people play.

Athletics provide a trial-by-fire ordeal, especially competitive sports like boxing and track and field. The safer society makes living, the more necessary those physical 'tests' are. Now that we have no more continents to discover or new oceans to chart, we turn to such esoteric activities as paddling across the Atlantic in a bathtub, or climbing Mt Everest blindfolded.

The trouble is – most young people (most people!) don't know what they're missing. Let's face it: few teenagers want school to be tougher, so that 'A's are rare as hen's teeth and failures are put back or kicked out. You don't realize that the reason you smartass the teacher or disrespect any authority is to take a risk, to test limits.

All we're suggesting is that you develop positive ways to test your worth, to establish your limits. Commit yourself to something, anything that involves risking failure – whether it's learning the guitar or pole-vaulting. Whatever it is, it should involve a sacrifice, giving up something, or else attainment isn't so sweet. An Olympic-bound swimmer swims laps morning, noon, and night, week in, week out, while his/her friends are just hangin' out. When you give up something, you work harder to make the loss 'worth' it. If you're going to give up all those movies and cokes and dates – you're damn well going to make it pay off. That's what commitment is. It starts with a decision, as opposed to just floating along and dabbling.

A commitment is essentially an agreement or contract you make with yourself. That's the only kind of commitment that matters. (Sometimes it helps to advertise your commitment to the outside world – to let them know what you've decided to do, to help you remain firm in your resolve.) We aren't talking about things you're supposed to do or expected to do, like get good grades or mow the lawn. We're talking about things you don't have to do, like becoming skateboard champ or the captain of the debating team.

When you commit yourself to a course of action that tests your mental and physical perseverance, and you hold true to that goal – you're going to come out a head taller. Even if you don't become a champion or the best at something…so long as *you* know you gave it your best. There is nothing to equal the sense of worth it produces. That is so rare these days.

Practically everyone holds back a little something, if only to protect their ego. If they 'fail,' they can always say, "Well, I could have been the best had I *really* tried." How many times can you say you put out 100% and gave it everything you had? When you only give 80%, you'll only get 80% back. Until you go all-out, you'll never know complete satisfaction. Giving 100% is the basis of pride, of self-esteem. People don't even love one another 100% (out of fear of being 'hurt'). Holding back is just cheating yourself. If you're going to stand in front of a microphone and sing – then, for God's sake, SING…let go absolutely. Don't try to protect yourself by holding something back. Even if 'winning' is all that counts with you, when you give 100% and you don't get applauded, at least you know where you stand.

People who only go halfway are always bothered with 'maybes.' "Maybe I could be great if I really tried." Well, if you really tried and you weren't great, then you'd know your limitations. Everyone has limitations. Limits are only troublesome when you don't know what they are, so you shoot too low or seek something that's beyond your talent or physical abilities. But you'll never know if you don't test your limits. And the only fair test is the one that stretches you.

Some limits are easier to establish than others. If you're into weight-lifting, it's easy to determine what weight is beyond your ability to press. Most physical tests fall into that black and white category. Either you can run a four-minute mile or you can't, at any point in time. It's the talent area that's more difficult to assess. This is where most people hold back. This is where it is tougher to let yourself go…to go for broke. But no performer ever attained greatness without giving 100% (which explains why there are so few great performers). Great talent is not rare. The world is full of talented people who *could be* great but won't be because they don't put out 100%.

Unrealized potential is such a waste. It's like wasting natural resources. And no matter how the possessors of that talent may rationalize the failure to realize their potential, the fact that they didn't is debilitating. It does terrible things to your self-esteem. Having talent is therefore something of a burden. You are obliged to utilize it.

To recap: our society tries to insulate people against failure by accepting half-hearted efforts. This leaves most of us untested and untried, which generates a lack of self-esteem. So we turn to things like clothes and cars to make up for the lack of self-confidence.

But the only meaningful achievement is personal. Something you've done that's as good as you can possibly do…after much trial and effort. You don't need money for that. You don't need under-standing parents or a good neighborhood. You don't need a good police force or a terrific minister. All you need is yourself. A will-ingness to commit yourself to doing something as good as you can do it. When you've done that, you've done all you can do. Win or lose – you'll be way ahead.

Notes to Myself

Notes to Myself

19

Wake Up

A New Age is dawning.

The time is nigh (if we don't nuke ourselves back into the Stone Age in the meantime) when the standards set by the Great Ones – Buddha, Jesus, Ghandi, Muhammed, Socrates, and Confucius – becomes every man's *modus operandi*. Our spiritual nature is gaining sway over man's brute side. Consider how far we've come in the last 500 years, much less 5000 years. Can you imagine a pack of Vikings rallying to halt the slaughter of seal pups, or a bunch of Elizabethans protesting the cutting of giant sequoia, or ancient Romans rising up in righteous indignation over an unjust war?

It is interesting to chart man's progress from our lumbering ancestors to our present elegance. Five centuries ago the great mass of humanity lived as peasants or slaves. It required dawn-to-dusk labor to half-fill their stomachs. Survival left no time and less desire to develop a higher consciousness, to wonder and reach for answers that didn't relate to food, sex, and warmth. When the Industrial Revolution brought a degree of leisure time to the masses, people had time to think about…thinking, which moved them closer to the angels and further from the animals.

This evolution from a bent over beast to *Homo sapiens'* present status is testimony that man, like Rome, wasn't built in a day …or even seven days. With every generation we become more refined.

Did you know that just 5,000 years ago (a mere tick on the evolutionary clock), civilized, sophisticated Greeks, Persians, Hindus, Chinese, could not recognize the color blue? It's true. Aristotle spoke of the tricolored rainbow. In the Bible, the Rig-Veda and Homer's epic poems, the sky is described thousands of times without one mention of blue. That's because color sense is a recently acquired human faculty, appearing in the race after the sense of shame and remorse (but before such as our musical sense – Herodotus couldn't carry a tune!).†

Unless you are an anthropologist, this is no big deal – except that it points to the fact that man is developing, being perfected.

---

†For more detailed information on this, see *Cosmic Consciousness: A Study in the Evolution of the Human Mind* by Richard M Bucke, MD, 19th Reprint, 1961, Citadel Press, Secaucus, NJ.

What *is* important for you to know is that not all of us are being perfected at the same rate. Somebody had to see blue before somebody else. Blueness didn't just happen to everyone simultaneously – as if God declared blue to exist and splashed it across the sky one morning so everyone could look up and exclaim, "Hallelujah, it's blue!" Because only a few saw blue before the many, early blue-seers surely had trouble relating what they saw to their blue-blind friends. (Maybe the first looney bins were filled with folk who babbled about blue.)

The faculty of morality is even more recently acquired than our color and musical senses. As a consequence, there are many people with no morality† and many more who are only partially moral.

Someone who is equipped with a well-developed conscience – a sense of right and wrong – presumes everyone else is similarly outfitted. Wrong. You will find yourself playing and competing with people who don't play by your (moral) rules. This can be awfully confusing and downright dangerous.

It is almost impossible for a compassionate/moral person to conceive how a seemingly normal man – one equipped with the

---

†Being without morals is being amoral. Immorality is acting contrary to what you know is right. So, only moral people can be said to be immoral.

same features and attributes – can coolly torture another human being or commit other overt acts of premeditated cruelty to their own kind (much less to dumb animals). Anyone who would casually stick red hot pins in some wretch's eyeballs is *not* like you; he only looks like you. He lacks compassion: the ability to transfer his feelings to another person's experience.

So it is that the moral person is easy prey for amoral people. And it is quite impossible to judge who is playing by which rules. Many people who lack morality regularly attend church and mouth pious platitudes about 'right' action. (After all, they don't realize they're amoral!) But when things get rough and turn against them they'll lie, cheat, even kill to protect themselves… and not bat an eye.

This explanation won't change your shock or surprise when someone shows themselves to be amoral. But it does explain how some people can be sooo bad.

All the above bears testimony that the Age of Aquarius (akin to heaven on Earth) is a-comin'. It will not be long before all of us possess a moral sense; when we are incapable of doing unto others what we would not have done unto us. Fast on the heels of that evolutionary plateau will come the ultimate faculty, cosmic consciousness. Some few individuals possess this now –

about as many as could see blue in Homer's time! What one has, all will have. Today's exception will be tomorrow's rule. It is inevitable – just a matter of time.

Notes to Myself

20

The Future Is Not
What It Used to Be

A preview of coming attractions.

You just finished reading about the 'New Age' that's dawning.

But don't let that lull you into thinking this millennium is an automatic, can't miss sure-thing.

We may be on the threshold of the so-called Aquarian Age, but that threshold has two doors facing it. One door opens to heaven on Earth, accompanied by the "Hallelujah Chorus." The other door leads to Doomsday. Which is which?

You and your friends will be the ones who decide. If it's excitement you want – being involved in momentous events – you couldn't have picked a better time to grow up. This is the first time in human history we've had the means for destroying both ourselves and our planetary habitat. And at the same time we've never been so close to elevating ourselves above the animal kingdom into the spiritual realm.

All the chips will be on the table when it's your turn to step up and play. Every hope that ever has been hoped, every prayer that ever has been sent heavenward, every pain every martyr has ever suffered, every battle won and lost along the way to the present, every lesson ever learned, every bite of every meal, every kind thought and compassionate act, every poem ever penned, every word spoken over the countless centuries – all this will be made meaningless or meaningful by the actions taken or not taken by your generation. (If it's responsibility you want – you'll get all you can handle, and then some!)

We've lived with the threat of nuclear war hanging over our heads for some time now. And while that won't go away as long as our commanders need enemies to remain in command, we won't use the specter of a nuclear holocaust to awaken you to the responsibilities you are about to be burdened with. There are new threats to our existence that can't be lived with, not even another twenty-five years.

The destruction of the ozone layer won't snuff out the human race (PFFFTT!) like that! But unless the depletion of this layer of atmosphere that protects our hide from the sun's ultravio-

let rays ceases instanter, you'd better start digging yourself a bur-
row and learn to like living underground forevermore.

Then there is the much-ballyhooed, 'greenhouse' effect
whereby the polar ice caps melt to change the face of our globe
socially, politically, economically, and geographically. (When was
the last time a new generation was confronted with that kind of
challenge?) Sure, ice caps have melted before, but the causes were
natural, as in gradual. Anyway, humans weren't around then to
live with the consequences. ('Live' is a poor word choice – 'sink or
swim' better describes the consequences.)

There are other Armageddon-size threats you'll be facing,
but the purpose of this chapter isn't to make you fearful. Quite the
contrary – these global problems contain the seeds of your salva-
tion. Consider...

Until recently, all mankind's problems (all except 'human
nature'!) were localized. A famine here, pestilence there, a horrible war in one place, terrible tyranny another place. As long as
it isn't our place, as long as it is the Ethiopians who are starving,
or the Russians who are oppressed, or the Jews who are slaughtered the problem can be lived with. A perfect example is found
in the AIDS plague. As long as it was thought to be a homosexual
problem, it wasn't our problem. Now, suddenly, AIDS has crossed
the tracks to the straight side of town where its grabbed main-

stream America by the throat. So now it's become everyone's problem. What a difference that makes! There's nothing like a common threat to create a common concern and a common determination to solve it. (Look up the word, 'commonweal.') Apparently that's what it takes to make us realize we are all in this together; it's one for all and all for one...or all for naught.

Now that the whole world, and all the life forms that inhabit it, are threatened equally and simultaneously with extinction, one of two scenarios will take place:

One, we will continue to squabble over whose fault it is, and who should do what about it...until there is no one left to blame or fight with.

Or, two, we will drop our differences forthwith and join together in a common, global effort to undo what our differences have done.

It's a damned shame we have to be pushed to the brink of extinction before recognizing we're all God's children – one vineyard nourishes all. Let us hope the light dawns before we are over the edge and falling. Then it will do no good to cling to the rocks falling with us.

Footnote: Years ago, in the 1950s sometime, there was a second-rate sci-fi flick with a first-rate plot. With apologies to the author, to whom we can't give due credit for the lack of a remembered title, the story went like this: an advanced alien culture from another galaxy (why do all 'advanced alien cultures' seem to be from 'another galaxy', when the Milky Way is a perfectly good galaxy?) sent an emissary to warn our globe's warring nations to make peace, lest our terrestrial arguments ignite a nuclear war whose backlash would upset the equilibrium of other galaxies. Well, of course, you know what happened next: the world's leaders gathered, as ordered, to hear the emissary's ultimatum. As soon as they heard it, each leader began defending his country and blaming the others. The inter-galactic messenger issued a cosmic 'shut-up' and proceeded to read them the galactic riot act: "Set aside your gratuitous gripes and petty peeves from this moment onward, or you shall be annihilated without another word of warning." Too bad we can't have peace on Earth by proclamation. But next best is a clear and present danger, such as a high tide that turns the Pentagon into an island.

Notes to Myself

Notes to Myself

21

Do Something,
For a Change

When you pray for potatoes, pick up a hoe.

The last chapter dumped all the problems that have accumulated over the millennia, all (wo)man's hopes and aspirations, right in your lap. It isn't the first time the incoming generation has been saddled with the outgoing generation's failures; although it may be the last time! It's almost one of the standard rites of passage to have the weight of the world placed on the shoulders of each succeeding generation. ("If once you don't succeed – try, try again.")

The preceding chapter's bottom line was this: the problems won't fix themselves...and if you don't fix them, there'll be no one left to fix them. *We've come to the end of line, and look who's standing there!?* Also it was said you are up to the task...if you all pull together.

There you have it. Your generation either will be human-kind's all-time *numero-uno* HERO, or the generation that presided over *Homo sapiens'* final demise. The doomsday option, it must be said, is easiest to accomplish: all you have to do is *nothing*. The Hero's role will take some doing; including the cooperation of all races, creeds, colors and political persuasions.

Do not allow the enormity of the task to stop you. Epic journeys are completed one step at a time...starting with the first step. For inspiration, study the Dark Ages. They were no picnic. But look what they led to, *the Renaissance*. Talk about break-throughs! It was as if humankind had been held prisoner in the cave of its birth. Only we didn't realize we were imprisoned so there was no escape. Then, all of a sudden, there appeared a pin-point of light – but in the blackness that was the Dark Ages, it blazed like a beacon. The huddled multitudes rose and staggered towards the illumination – like moths to a bright bulb – and suddenly found themselves outside their cave in a totally new world full of light.

So, too, can your generation be the torchbearer that leads your children out of the gully of gloom and guilt – up to a higher level of existence (from which vantage point you will experience dimensions we've been blind to).

According to the Scriptures, "the children will lead us."
The wisdom behind that ancient writ was touched on earlier:
"Teenagers are a lot closer to making their lives work than anyone
else...closer by virtue of not having had time to get very far off course."

The adult world will sniff and snort at the very suggestion
that you, a bunch of snotty-nosed, self-indulgent kids could save
the world.

Ignore those naysayers (remembering what a mess they've
made of things). You can do it. *Write history rather than repeat it.*
It's not all that difficult, really. Just remain conscious of that objective, speak of it, act on it. Be the initiator. You will attract con-
verts by example. A few will become many.

To succeed does not require keeping score. There'll be no
missing the New Age when it arrives. Breakthroughs are not slow,
gradual turnarounds. Going from medieval darkness to a radiant
renaissance was not an agonizing, inch-at-a-time process, but a
sudden, glorious burst of spontaneous energy – a blossoming, an-
nounced with blaring trumpets and the applause of millions.

Martin Luther King, Jr, knew it would happen like that –
not miraculously, but produced by the accumulation of all the
right thoughts and actions to date. Fear and suspicion will disap-

pear, virtually overnight. Our enemies will be revealed as shadows...our own shadows! Who needs weapons then? Who needs walls, borders, threats, and coercion? The sun shines on everyone.

The energy that fuels change accumulates slowly...at first. But your generation has inherited almost a full tank! You have only to add one more drop. So what are you waiting for? *Do something, for a change.*

Apologia

This is not the sort of stuff that should be included in a manual for teenagers. (If this book were written twenty-five years ago it would have been without this chapter as well as the preceding one!) Asking a teenager to turn away from the mirror, drop his books and skip Friday night's party to mount the barricades and defend the world against the forces of evil is asking a lot – probably too much, considering what's already on your plate. Even if you don't answer this call to arms now – for which you are forgiven – there still will be time when 18 rolls around and you have the right to vote. Then you *must* answer the call. Nothing could be more important. Jobs, affluence, freedom, love, the quality of your life – life itself – depend on your actions. Action follows thought. So start thinking, in preparation for doing something, for a change. If you don't, history will repeat itself...only this time, there'll be no repeat performance. You'll be the last act!

Notes to Myself

Notes to Myself

22

Mopping Up

Bits 'n' pieces too short to call chapters, too good to throw out.

Intuition: What it is and isn't and why you can depend on the real thing.

The dictionary defines 'intuition' as knowing without being able to trace the source of the knowing. Well, that definition will have to be updated in the light of recent research. It seems that the thing we've been calling intuition turns out to be a facet of the nervous system. It's an 'it'! Maybe now you'll trust it.

It really makes no difference to us non-scientists how the intuition works. What matters is that it works! Your intuition can't be wrong.

And yet we all have heard cases where intuitive 'voices' prompted someone to kill or destroy. But that isn't the intuition speaking. Impulses push you into wrong action. An impulse tends to be wishful thinking, a kind of hallucination.

No one can tell you if the voice you hear is an echo of your desires or your intuition (only one of which is telling you straight). If your past is pebbled with problems, chances are you should ignore the voice that whispers in your ear. If everything is working out for you – trust it.

The voice of intuition doesn't rationalize; doesn't weigh the pluses and minuses. Your intuitive voice is confident, certain – it doesn't mince words. It comes from deep-down inside. It is the sound of you.

The 'Beginner's Mind'

The 'beginner's mind' is a phrase taken from Eastern philosophy which means total receptivity to what is happening in one's experience.

That's one (of the few) advantages a teenager has over grown-ups. Experience tends to program people, set up preconceived notions about the way something is supposed to turn out rather than allowing it to unfold – being open to any possibility.

When you have collected a past thirty or forty years long it is difficult to keep an open mind, but not impossible. So-called 'creative' people welcome the unexpected and do not feel threatened by the unknown. That's why painters and advertising copywriters and that ilk have a childlike quality about them. They are still full of the ol' Gee Whiz.

Harmony

The highest and best use of this life experience surely is to live in harmony with your fellows and environment. That is, in fact, the very meaning of cosmos: a universe in harmony.

The basic stuff of the universe – atoms – is a study in harmony, as is that granddaddy of all atoms, the galaxies.

Someone who has been illumined by cosmic consciousness has had the transcending experience of feeling/being an integral part of the All.

All kinds of good flows from 'living in harmony': peace, freedom, good health, the ability to enjoy others. People with this quality are nice to be around, so they have lots of friends; everything comes easy for them.

Living in harmony does not mean everyone marches to the same drummer. Harmony is a blending, an assembly of different notes and values that together create a pleasing effect. So harmony allows for the offbeat and discordant.

All together now…

Patience

High technology, and especially TV, has made us addicts for instant gratification. We see lifetimes compressed into thirty-minute segments. Jets flash us across a continent; a trip that required three months of unimaginable hardship for our great-grandparents. So naturally we expect everything to happen like (snap) that! And if it doesn't – forget it – life is too short.

That's unfortunate. It means too many people will never learn to play the piano, never climb Kilimanjaro or become neurosurgeons. Personal accomplishment still takes as long as ever. Skills are not learned in a day. Talent is not developed overnight.

Another reason for our impatience is that we have so much to choose from. It used to be that if your father was a stonemason, you'd be a stonemason – there was no choice. Coal miners' sons became coal-miners and the offspring of gentry were destined to be gentry.

Today we face what might be called 'a misery of choice.' A stonemason's son can grow up to be a labor leader. A shopkeeper's offspring can become a rock star. The mighty can fall and the fallen can rise. Because we can be anything, we tend to back away from something that takes perseverance, thinking that if one thing doesn't work out there'll be something else.

Adolescent Stress

As covered in Chapter 1, adolescence is a highly stressful period of development. Physical, social, and psychological changes occur simultaneously. Many teenagers respond to all this complexity by withdrawing – either by slumping into passivity or becoming rebellious.

When adults – parents, teachers, other authorities – try to help, the over-stressed teenager is apt to react in a way that causes the adult to get angry, frustrated, and intolerant. And that, of course, is what you were hoping for – it's your way of overcoming that helpless feeling. "Look! I'm able to drive my parents up the wall."

'Maladjusted' behavior is based on inherited criteria; that is, what's 'wrong' is based on what society considers 'right.' Kids can be locked up, force-fed pills and suffer endless hours on some shrink's couch because of antisocial behavior. Yet if that same kid were born into a family of Laplanders his problems wouldn't be noticed, or if they were – he'd get a swift kick in the butt and that would be the end of it.

This is not to treat teenage ills lightly. Suicides among teenagers have tripled in just this past decade. And most of these tragedies happen in the affluent suburbs, not in the (hopeless)

ghettos. Shocking, to say the least. Why? It's not guilt. Punks
don't feel guilty about being punky. The basic problem is a lack of
meaning to their lives – a 'who cares' or 'why care' attitude. That
had its beginning after President Kennedy was gunned down.
President Nixon's Watergate scandal didn't do a lot to put meaning and values back into a young person's life. So the attitude is –
why turn the corner if it leads to that?

It is hoped that the preceding chapters will encourage you
to *press on, regardless*; to turn that corner and move on to something that will encourage others to follow.

When you get down in the dumps, and are convinced you
have nothing to live for, the best way to snap out of those dol-
drums and revive your enthusiasm is to exercise. When you're rid-
ing your bike full-tilt, drilling a soccer ball past the goalie, or jog-
ging mile after mile you are not thinking downer thoughts; you
are totally involved in doing. Exercise pumps you up, gets you
breathing deep, feeds oxygen into your bloodstream. Nothing lifts
the mood better than that, and improves your health in the bar-
gain. So instead of jumping off the Tallahassee bridge, run, kick,
hit, jump, throw, catch – get up off your ass and swing into action.
That *never* fails to make you feel good.

The best of times, the worst of times

In the dingy Dark Ages, people didn't go around bitching about "these terrible times." People didn't expect anything but what they got: hunger, disease, misery, hopelessness.

Today we expect such a lot. We expect to work a little and earn *mucho*. We expect never to go hungry, never to be treated unjustly. We expect to be well educated and well housed. Not that everyone is. But everyone expects it – thanks to the movies, TV, jet travel, and satellite communications.

Our expectations are also the product of mankind's stunning progress from brute to demigod. As heaven on Earth becomes a conceivable reality, anything that is less than heavenly is 1) noticed, and 2) resented. So we are rightly upset when some tinhorn generalissimo tortures a few of his disloyal subjects. But no such hue and cry would have been raised just fifty years ago.

John Lennon was right back in '67 when he wrote, ". . . it's getting bettah, getting bettah all the time. . ." And the more we expect, the better it will get.

There are some who say we are trying to progress too fast; to redress too many grievances too soon. Blacks, Chicanos, Haitians, the elderly, Vietnam vets, American Indians, Palestinians, Armenians, Cubans, everyone is shouting, pushing and shoving to get their due, and complaining bitterly when it is denied them. And their wails are heard by all, thanks to electronic media. So we get the idea that there is so much – maybe more than ever – injustice around us, so many wrongs to be righted.

Yet the fact is – never has there been more effort to help the helpless, with all kinds of positive results to show for it. Indians are given back their land. Cubans are given a home. Asians find refuge. Minorities are receiving a much better education. Women get better pay and equal access. The light of world opinion makes it increasingly difficult to repress human rights. There is much left to be done, God knows. But it is happening – now more than ever, faster than ever. It's as if the great mass of humanity had been feeling its way for centuries through a pitch-black, seemingly endless tunnel. Every inch has been an agony. Only some inner spark lighted any hope and pushed one foot ahead of the other. Now, suddenly, a point of light is seen shining up ahead. The end of the tunnel is in sight!

Do you think so much humanity so long starved of hope will be content to continue shuffling slowly towards freedom? Hell no! A roar goes up and everyone stampedes for the exits!

And those who have been in charge of man's groping progress now find their orders, threats, and entreaties have little effect.
They are ignored, derided, and run-over. That's because they are
no longer needed to lead the way. Now the people can see where
they want to be. They also see that their old warders – the gener-
als, presidents, industrialists, bankers, policemen, even ministers –
stand between them and their expectations. Trouble is, the Old
Guard is operating with its back to the future. To them it appears
that people have lost their minds, rushing ahead shouting "Gimme,
gimme, gimme."

No doubt the first taste of freedom causes people to act badly.
Prison breaks are not exactly an orderly process. So you hear a lot
of tsk-tsking about how outstretched hands turn to fists. Sure, minorities have more civil rights than they did one hundred fifty
years ago, but they want it even better; a predictable reaction to
success, and a sure sign that things are getting better all the time.

Thrillaholics

Psychologists have discovered that some people need thrills as diabetics need insulin. These congenital thrill-seekers are not necessarily braver or more courageous than we who are fearful of high-risk diversions. The reason they love high speed, falling out of airplanes, hanging upside down in amusement parks and other forms of torment is a neurological need for the biochemical state that is produced by intense excitement. They have an imbalance of a brain chemical called monoamine oxidaze, which causes depression. Risk and fear seem to change the levels of that chemical, lifting them from torpor to elation. In other words, being scared to death makes them feel alive!

So don't think you're a fraidycat to avoid horror movies, rollercoasters or steep mountainsides covered with slippery snow. You don't need a shot of monoamine oxidaze. They do.

Give and get

People who always give of themselves and their property
don't do it because it hurts. Quite the contrary. It makes them
feel good! They receive an immediate payback, an injection of
self-esteem.

Young people have spent most of their years receiving. You
receive food, shelter, clothing, medical care, and love. (Some of
you receive more, some less.) Society gives you an education,
roads, sewers, and protection...without asking anything in return.

Lately, there's a movement afoot to give you an opportunity
to give – in order to receive the glow produced by selfless service
to others. Like so many new ideas, this one was first planted in
California by a State Legislature Panel on Self-Esteem. This au-
gust panel turned around and created the Human Corps Task
Forces on all the state's four-year public campuses. College students are asked to perform community service an average of thirty
hours a year. This produced the Community Involvement Center
at San Francisco State University, YES at Humbolt State, and
similar groups at UC Berkeley and at Stanford. What about your
campus, high school?

Of course you can give of yourself individually. Wherever you live, you're surrounded with people who need help – especially elderly people. Just being around young people makes their old bones feel better. The phone book is full of places that care for the elderly. They are always understaffed and would welcome your helping hands.

Anytime is a good time to give time. But the very best time is when you yourself are having a bad time. When you spend time helping others, there's no time to feel sorry for yourself.

The Global Village

This book is not addressed to San Francisco kids, or California kids, or American kids. Today's kids belong to a larger community, the 'global village'...a village created by TV, computers, telecommunications and supersonic travel.

The realization of this may be some time in catching up to the reality, but the generation that follows you will consider kids in the Balkans (you do know where the Balkans are, don't you?) as much a part of their scene as kids from another state are now.

This enlarged sense of community will help wipe out borders and other arbitrary differences that promote wars. It will also give rise to a collective consciousness that is a zillion times more powerful than the sum total of the individuals it comprises.

Speak up

In case you hadn't noticed, teenagers aren't the greatest communicators. Oh, you do okay when it comes to intramural conversation, which involves non-verbal forms of communication; that is, lotsa body language. And like all affinity groups, teenagers develop their own secret language (which is unique to each generation, locale and lifestyle†), the purpose of which is to avoid communicating with outsiders; e.g., non-teenagers. But when you're standing on the carpet facing a disapproving parent, a disbelieving teacher – officialdom of any sort – you seldom receive a fair hearing. Because what they hear and what you mean and feel don't jibe! Audiences comprised of your elders are intimidating, critical.

You are expected to speak their language, to communicate on their terms. They will seldom pause to translate; to interpret your monosyllables and jargon.

That legendary 'generation gap' is really a communications gap. Adults don't respect what you say because of the way you say it. Most times they don't even hear you! A conversation with your elders too often begins and ends with a statement/edict/proclama-

---

† *Blacks have theirs, as do jazz musicians, gays, lawyers, New Englanders, admen, conservatives, Communists, medical people, aluminum siding salesmen, et al.*

tion from them. They may appear to be listening when you respond, but they have decided, more or less unconsciously, to discount your reply. It is rare when anyone from the other side of 30 listens with interest and respect to your views.

This is just one of the many frustrations that come from looking grown-up and acting your age. The only way to change it is to stop acting your age; in other words, sound old for your age. There's nothing that impresses the father of your date so much as an earnest young man who volunteers his concern over this month's record trade deficit. Those of you who either can't or won't play that game are inclined to do the opposite: to be unforthcoming, never volunteer anything, act sullen, mumble, focus your eyes downward. That puts an end to those one-way conversations.

No wonder young people prefer their own company. To avoid know-it-all adults you close ranks, form tight little inner circles as a way to keep out discordant elements – anyone who doesn't look like you, talk like you, think like you, act like you. That may make you feel secure, but it sure doesn't let you in for new experiences, ideas. Subcultures are comfortable...and stifling! A bunch of closed-minded people agreeing with themselves, reinforcing fondly held prejudices.

Beware of these incestuous affinity groups. Sure, they make life less threatening. But they also make it terribly boring and predictable and repetitious. But the worst thing about getting stuck into some tight little circle – it doesn't encourage you to be you, it doesn't allow you to be you; to gain a sense of your own unique uniqueness. The ability to communicate, to express your self, requires you to know your self; to be your self. Your self is not a jock, or a Latino, a tough guy, a pretty girl, a skinhead. You are one of a kind, like a snowflake is one of a kind (snowfields notwithstanding!).

Time

Time didn't start ticking the minute you were born.

Everything's new when you're new: every sight, sound, experience, realization.

Your first kiss, as far as you're concerned, is the very first kiss ever kissed!

You discover a new word and presume it's new to everyone else. Indeed, with each new discovery, the discoverer is wont to stake a claim to it. But before you go running out into the street shouting, "Eureka! I have found it," remember – what's new to you is old to most of the rest of the world. Whatever you have imagined, conceived, or thought of, has most likely been imagined, conceived, and thought of many times before you.

This is not said to put down your discoveries. Far from it. You should be thrilled and delighted with each new encounter made along life's path – while knowing several billion minds have been busy before yours began its quest.

Of course, every once in a great while you may in fact be first to do something, especially in the field of science and sports.

In such cases, you do become the beginning point. If you can't manage that, try inventing a 'first.' For example, you could be first to fly a purple kite with a green tail over the Grand Canyon on a Sunday morning whilst singing "Down in the Valley." Bring along a friend to record the event in case it qualifies for the *Guiness Book of World Records*.

What if…

We waste an unholy amount of time applying hindsight to current events that affect us negatively. When something turns out bad, our imaginations rush to undo the event with 'what if's, reconstructing the negative outcome to produce a different result. If it's an automobile accident, we go back a couple of blocks before the crash and wish we had missed one or more stoplights… which would have meant missing the truck that we in fact hit. Or, "If only I turned left on Third Avenue as I usually do instead of going straight on Main Street." Yes, and had we stayed in bed another ten minutes this morning, that truck would not have been there when you crossed the intersection.

There's no end to such musings. "What if we hadn't moved to California last year?" "What if Mom and Dad had never been married?" "What if the Earth settled in an orbit a couple of million miles closer to the sun?"

Once an occurrence occurs, it could not have occurred any other way, with any other result. What is, is. What isn't, isn't. There are no 'might have beens,' no other possibilities possible. The 'what if's only make you feel unlucky. We might better consider how it might have been worse. Included in those infinite "What ifs…" are innumerable possiblities that might have killed or maimed you; for instance, if you had reached that intersection one minute earlier, you would have collided with a speeding fire engine! How many times have you missed being mugged, hit by a stray bullet, being aboard an aircraft that exploded in mid-air, *ad nauseam*? Count your blessings.

Drop-outs lose out

A University of California study found drop-outs are twice as likely to lose their jobs than high school graduates, and four times more likely than college grads. The UC study also reports that each additional year of secondary school reduces by 35% the chance you'll end up in the welfare line. What's more, earning a high school diploma reduces your chances of being arrested by 90%. (Nearly 60% of all jail inmates did not complete high school!)

It's too late for the tens of millions who have already dropped out of school in the last decade. But it's not too late for you. Think long and hard before you follow their footsteps. Dropping out is not the easy way out.

Another report on the same subject paints an equally black picture for dropouts. Only 14% of new jobs in the US can be filled by people with less than a high school education. And most of those jobs are menial, manual employment that lead nowhere and pay very little. This report goes on to say 52% of the new jobs that will be available until 1995 will require some college, while only 38% of the future workforce are in fact attending college. Obviously, the United States is facing a severe shortage of educated workers; a lack that will crimp the competitive status of American business and industry. Because most other industrialized nations have no such shortage of well-educated workers, they will take up the slack caused by our social and educational system.

The real dummy here is the United States of America. This country should go back to school to study Socio-economics 1A. That teaches it's far more cost-effective to educate the economically-deprived than it is to shut down factories and build bigger jails. There's no profit in punishment.

Teenage Rights

Not only do teenagers have rights, legal rights – you have your very own Youth Law Center, located in San Francisco.

According to this resource, nearly half the states in the US (including California, Illinois, Indiana, and Texas) have so-called "Child Emancipation" laws that permit a court to declare that a child is grown-up before he or she reaches 18. This law requires the court, when petitioned by a minor, to determine if 1) the child can manage his or her finances, 2) whether emancipation is in the child's best interests, and 3) whether the parents agree to emancipation. (If the parents don't agree, emancipation is more legally complicated.)

Dependent minors who run afoul of the law and end up in a reform school or juvenile detention center also have certain rights requiring separation from violent and adult detainees. You have a right to certain health services; access to family, friends, and legal aid. Your rights also cover proper exercise and recreation, food, heat, light, clothing, and a place to sleep. Nor can you be restrained by the use of handcuffs, shackles and isolation except in the most unusual circumstances. Your rights include protection from assault by other inmates.

Also, you have 'rights' when it comes to school discipline. As the level of punishment increases – so do your rights.

More details can be obtained from your community's Legal Aid society.

Better SADD than sorry

Fifty years ago, teenagers lost friends to things like diphtheria, tuberculosis, poliomyelitis, and 101 other diseases—all of which immunization has eliminated. Today, it's alcohol and mind-altering drugs, mixed with 3,000 lbs. of speeding steel, that kills young people.

No town, neighborhood or school is immune to this tragedy. There's no inoculation that'll make a drunk driver a safe driver. The only preventive medicine is called abstinence. When that fails, the last remaining remedy is to prevent the drinker from driving. By persuasion if possible. If that doesn't move the driver out of harm's way, then remove yourself as a passenger. A lousy way to end an evening. But consider the alternative!

Many times the driver won't give up the wheel and the passengers won't get out because it's a long, cold walk home. Asked why they didn't call their folks for help, most teenagers roll their eyes and shrug their shoulders—by way of saying "Are you kidding? I'd rather take my chances on the road." You obviously don't think your parents will take kindly to being awakened in the wee hours for chauffeur duty. Nor are your parents overjoyed to hear you're with a bunch of drunks.

An organization exists to eliminate that 'reason' for driving and drinking. Students Against Drunk Driving (SADD) has developed a "Contract For Life" for parents and teenagers. You agree not to drink and drive or be driven by anyone who has – calling your parents for a ride home, whatever the hour, however far. Your parents agree not to blame or punish or even bitch if you call for assistance.

This contract has served to remove many a zonked-out driver from behind the wheel. And when the driver won't cooperate, you can remove yourself from his car without having to make the long walk home. For some copies of their contract, write SADD, 110 Pleasant Street, Corbin Plaza, Marlboro, MA 01752, or for faster action call (617) 481-3568. If your school hasn't introduced the student body to this SADD program, make it your crusade to do so.

Thought-Release Capsules

Love

True love doesn't bind, it frees.

"Loving yourself will dissolve your ego; you will feel no need to prove you are superior. And the more loving you are, the more loving are those around you. Play a happy tune and happy dancers will join you."

—The Lazy Man's Guide to Enlightenment

"Peace can only be made by those who are peaceful, and love can only be shown by those who love."

—Alan Watts

If you learn to love, you will do all things well.

Trust

"He who does not trust enough will not be trusted."

—Lao-tsu

"Trust the Universe. Do not feel diminished by its immensity. The cosmos bears witness to your immensity, for you are it and it is you."

—Alan Watts

Money

"Money is a terrible master but an excellent servant."

—PT Barnum

No one knows how to deal with the person who wants only money.

"Blessed are the young, for they shall inherit the national debt."

—Herbert Hoover

"Young people, nowadays, imagine that money is everything, and when they grow older they know it."

—Oscar Wilde

"Work is the price you pay for money."   —Anonymous

Success & Failure

"I cannot give you a formula for success, but I can give you the formula for failure: try to please everybody."

—Herbert Bayard Swope

"Success often comes from taking a misstep in the right direction."

—Anonymous

"The most important single ingredient in the formula of success is knowing how to get along with people."

—Theodore Roosevelt

"Be awful nice to 'em goin' up, because you're gonna meet 'em all comin' down."   —Jimmy Durante

"Show me a good loser and I'll show you a loser."

—Jimmy Carter

"'Trying' is another word for 'failing.'"

—HSC

Possessions

"…not collecting treasures prevents stealing. Not seeing desirable things prevents confusion of the heart."

"…Amass a store of gold and jade, and no one can protect it."

"He who knows he has enough is rich."

—Lao-tsu

Honesty

"It is the honest man who admits to telling the occasional fib."

—HSC

"Truth gets you high. Lies bring you down."

—Ram Dass

Opposition

"A certain amount of opposition is a great help for a man. Kites rise against and not with the wind."

—John Neal

"Opposites create a worthwhile tension. Any structure (whether physical in nature or institutional, as in governmental structure) will collapse without tension. Cultures and empires dissolve be-cause of success (the absence of tension). It is opposition that cre-ates balance and harmony. Without the nays to balance the ayes equilibrium is lost, which is why tyrannies are short-lived."

—HSC

All can see beauty as beauty only because there is ugliness. All can know good as good only because there is evil.

"That which shrinks must first expand. That which fails must first be strong. That which is cast down must first be raised. Before re-ceiving there must be giving. This is called perception of the na-ture of things."

—Lao-tsu

How To Be Miserable

1. Use 'I' as often as possible.
2. Always be sensitive to slights.
3. Be jealous and envious.
4. Trust no one.
5. Never forget a criticism.
6. Always expect to be appreciated.
7. Look for faults in others.
8. Don't give until you get.

Participating

"You can't play the game of life on the sidelines. You've got to get into it, commit yourself. Participating is to join the whole, to be with the whole. That's healthy."

—HSC

Health

"Every second, 2,500,000 red blood cells in your body are being destroyed, and 2,500,000 more are being created. The breakdown of old forms is needed for health. When you don't exercise, you don't break down enough red cells and some of the worn-out ones stay around. Then you wonder why you don't feel so good."

—George Leonard

Civics

"…leading yet not dominating, this is the Primal Virtue."

"The more laws and restrictions there are,
The poorer people become.
The sharper men's weapons;
The more trouble in the land.
The more ingenious and clever men are,
The more stranger things happen.
The more rules and regulations,
The more thieves and robbers."

"When the country is ruled with a light hand
The people are simple.
When the country is ruled with severity,
The people are cunning."

"Force is followed by loss of strength."

"Why are the people rebellious?
Because the rulers interfere too much."

—Lao-tsu

"Laws are like cobwebs, which may catch small files but let wasps
and hornets break through."

—Jonathan Swift

Violence & Anger

"Violence, whether on a mass scale or between individuals is what
happens when fear or anger interferes with communication.
When you are very angry or very fearful, your breath comes
short…it's difficult to speak, or to speak sensibly. You have lost
control. In frustration, you strike out. It's the last resort of humans
(the first for animals). The parent who punishes a child (or
threatens to) with physical force is 'saying' he's/she's lost the ability to communicate, which is to lose one's humanity."

—HSC

"Anger is just one letter short of 'Danger.'"

—Della Reese

SHHHH

Those who know, do not talk.

The quieter you become, the more you hear.

Just BE HERE NOW.

Whimsy

Where it's at is seldom where it seems to be.

Smoothing rough spots sometimes requires abrasives.

There are no exceptions to the rule that everyone likes to be an exception to the rule

It isn't our factory that's polluting the lake, it's all those dead fish.

"By the time a man realizes that maybe his father was right, he usually has a son who thinks he's wrong."

—Charles Wadsworth

Experts: those whose opinions agree with my own.

"He who hesitates is last."

—Mae West

No guts, no glory.

—Mens' Room, Stanford Business School

Philosophy

"Act the way you'd like to be and soon you'll be the way you act."

—Dr GW Crane

"Go as far as you can see and when you get there you'll see far-ther…"

—L Ron Hubbard

"People who like many things are most likable."

—HSC

"There is nothing good nor bad that thinking does not make."

"Words without thoughts never to Heaven go."

—Shakespeare

"The same soil nurtures all plant life, from the humble weed to the mighty sequoia."

"Our opinions of others are too often expressed in terms of what we don't like about them. This makes our ego think better of it-self. That's how the ego grows and dominates – by comparing."

"No one can hinder or hurt you; assist or help you without your agreement."

—HSC

"Beareth all things, believeth all things, hopeth all things, en-dureth all things."

—Paul of Tarsus

"Live life joyfully and as consciously as possible."

—Ram Dass

Stay Foolish.

"It's no use to cling to rocks that are falling with you."

—Alan Watts

…misfortune comes from having a body. Without a body and its partner, the ego, how could there be misfortune?

"Training is everything. The peach was once a bitter almond; cauliflower is nothing but cabbage with a college education."

—Mark Twain

Philosophy

Forever is a longtime, but not as long as it was yesterday.

"It is only when you are pursued that you become swift."

—Kahlil Gibran

Be Aware: stay conscious of your consciousness.

"God gives the nuts, but He does not crack them."

—Proverb

He who searches for God has found him.

ETC ETC

THE PRESENT is the only thing that has no end.

PURPOSE? What purpose does a Universe of a million galaxies serve?

"HUMOR is a saving grace. True humor is the ability to laugh at one's self."

—HSC

"HAPPINESS is accepting what is."

—Werner Erhard

LIFE is celebration.

"YOU CAN NO LONGER DECEIVE YOURSELVES
AS YOU DID BEFORE.
YOU NOW HAVE GOT THE TASTE OF TRUTH."

—Ouspensky

Index

Index

Index

Afterword

Now that the end is here, the author is going to break the rule that's eliminated his 'I' person from all the preceding pages. That's because I wish to congratulate you. And well you deserve to be saluted.

Look what a lot of territory you've covered: 231 pages jam-packed with new thoughts, wild ideas, provocative precepts; con-troversial concepts about emotionally-charged subjects like how-to-save-the-world-without-even-trying, highs and lows, life and death, heaven and hell, S-E-X, parents, school, drugs, what makes you tick – none of it written in teenage jargon (which changes too fast to publish!).

If you can relate to even half of what's been laid down, you deserve an 'A.'

You're not expected to do anything in particular with what you've read, or even agree with any of it. The purpose of these pages is to put points of view on display – ways to cope and sur-vive; to grow and thrive. If you choose to reject this or that – fine. Terrific! Because you can't very well shoot down an idea without considering it – letting it into your consciousness. And every time your consciousness opens to let in something new, it expands, becomes more flexible, more aware. That's what the world needs – more awareness, more open minds.

"Kids won't read that stuff," I was warned. "You're wasting your time."

"Kids read their own mail, don't they?" I replied, and continued writing, hoping you did.

The answer to that is the tens of thousands of copies that have found their way to teenagers via schools, grandparents, local libraries, churches, detention centers, an anxious auntie and word of mouth.

There's more to it than that. There's more going on behind your eyes than meets the eye. Your interest and perception offers hope for the future...of this country, this race, this planet and the cosmos containing all of the above.

Of course, a hundred thousand perceptive readers is not exactly the whole world. Ah, but it is enough to change the world. A handful of enlightened young people are a force to be reckoned with! There are plenty of examples of a small cadre changing the course of human history, for better or for worse. Jesus and a few disciples changed the world for the better, whereas Hitler and his gaggle of crazed cronies gave the world two black eyes.

Which gets me to the point of this whole publishing effort: to help actualize a breakthrough – whereby mankind takes a quantum leap forward to a higher level of consciousness en route to the ultimate objective, heaven on Earth, a state of grace that is only possible when everyone treats everyone else as they would be treated themselves.

That will happen sooner or later (if mankind doesn't trip over its technology in the meantime), whether or not anyone reads these paragraphs. But on the chance a few well-chosen words can hasten that day, they should be writ!

Homo sapiens has made such leaps before. Going from the Dark Ages into *the Renaissance* was one. It had a trigger. As will the upcoming breakthrough.

Possibly, just maybe, your generation will be the one to write history instead of repeating, repeating, repeating it. All it takes is an enlightened elite…leadership that inspires without dominating. Might not the readers of these pages be such avatars, lighting the way to that higher level of consciousness? You have all the necessary qualifications.

When it does happen, there will be no missing it. Such breakthroughs are not slow, gradual transitions. They are bounding leaps, cosmic bridges leading from darkness to radiance – not inch by inch but in a sudden burst of energy; a spiritual blossoming that can turn cannons into plowshares. It will lead to a moral rearmament – a society of equals dedicated to the upgrading of the human mind, body and spirit. It can and will happen in one generation, if not today, some day. When it does, it will be no miracle but what happens when an accumulation of all the right thoughts and actions becomes so dense, it explodes with a force greater than the sum of its parts. The fallout will shower 'cosmic consciousness' on us all, illuminating the dark corners of the past.

Some might think this means the Second Coming. Whatever it is, that great day will dawn the moment self-esteem gains dominion over no-esteem...when there are more people who basically like themselves than there are who wish to hide from themselves.

That day is a-comin.' Anything you can do to hasten it will be very much appreciated. (What exactly you have to 'do,' or be, I'm sure I don't know; probably nothing more than to remain aware of that goal. That should do it.)

In any case, it's your world. Make the most of it.

About the Author

Mr Coombs has participated in the so-called consciousness raising movement since it first flowed out of the East to enter the mainstream of Western life in the early 1960's. The author interrupted a blooming advertising career (he was president of a large Westcoast ad agency) to launch the first public service communications agency serving non-profit organizations.

Mr Coombs has served on the Board of Directors of Intersection, a center for religion and arts, and acted as Communications Chairman for the Council of Churches. He has written a book *Edgework*, about dangerous avocations and another titled, *Press on Regardless*: the book for people who are new at being old.

The author was the Co-Founder of the Centers for Teenage Discovery which pioneered video theater workshops for teens. The author is a native of Northern California from where he roamed to reside in the Bahamas, Hawaii, Santa Monica. Now back in San Francisco "the least imperfect city in the world" he divides his time between the advertising business and producing a series of books on San Francisco and Gold Rush history.

Readers
Service
Center

(Re)Ordering Teenage Survival Manual

Retail booksellers should order from their wholesaler or from our distributors, DeVorss & Co., P.O.Box 550, Marina Del Rey, CA 90294; telephone: 213/870-7478.

Churches, non-profit organizations, public service agencies, schools/teachers, librarians and other professionals may purchase 3 or more copies at a 20% discount. Orders will be shipped postpaid.

Service clubs, youth organizations and companies who may wish to distribute quantities of the book as a premium or for fund-raising purposes should contact the publisher regarding quantity discounts.

Readers, whether ordering for yourself or others, may order direct from the publisher in the event the book is not available at local book stores. In such case, Discovery Books will forego the usual cost for "postage and handling."

Cash with order: Please include cheque or money order (made out to Discovery Books) with all orders.

Sales tax: If books are to be shipped to a California address, please add 6.5% sales tax.

ORDER FORM

Teenage Survival Manual

Please mail _____ books @ $9.95 each

$7.95 each *(professional price)*
see note previous page

NAME _____

STREET/P.O. _____

TOWN_____STATE ___ZIP _____

I enclose cheque/money order in the amount of $ _____
CA *residents add 6.5% sales tax. Make payable to Discovery Books* .

SPECIAL INSTRUCTIONS:
(NOTE HERE RECIPIENT'S NAME AND ADDRESS IF DIFFERENT FROM THAT GIVEN ABOVE.)

Mail your order to:
DISCOVERY BOOKS P.O. Box 410, Lagunitas, CA 94938
Thank you.

ORDER FORM

Teenage Survival Manual

Please mail _____ books @ $8.95 each _____
$0.75 each _____

NAME _____

STREET/PO. _____

TOWN _____ STATE _____ ZIP _____

I enclose check/money order in the amount of $ _____

SPECIAL INSTRUCTIONS

Mail your order:

DISCOVERY BOOKS, P.O. Box 1040, Escondido, CA 92025

Thank you.